ASPEN ON FOOT

Disclaimer

Wilderness and backcountry hiking involves potential risks. Hikers must be aware of dangers, assume personal responsibility and show respect for this untamed environment. The inclusion of a trail description in this guide does not imply that it is safe for you. Trails vary greatly in difficulty and require differing levels of physical conditioning and agility. Experience, equipment and weather are important variables. You can minimize risks to yourself and to your companions by being knowledgeable, prepared and alert.

The trail descriptions in this book are based on conditions experienced by the author in 1993 and 1994 and on information from topographic maps published by the U.S. Geological Survey. The author has made every effort to be precise and accurate. Despite this, many of the conditions described are subject to change from year to year and even from month to month. Your experiences on these trails may be unlike what is described. Brush Creek Books and the author do not warrant that the actual status of the trails will conform to the published descriptions and maps. The book is only a guide and should be supplemented with current information from a reliable local source.

The acquisition of a hiking guide does not make you an expert. Colorado hikers must be wary of volatile mountain weather and of the dangers of loose rock, swift water, snowfields and hidden precipices. A careless step or an unheeded thunderstorm can spell disaster. Brush Creek Books and the author assume no liability for injury or accident. Descriptions of these trails do not constitute an endorsement or recommendation.

ASPEN ON FOOT

Ruth Frey

Brush Creek Books

BRUSH CREEK BOOKS
1317 Livingston Street
Evanston, Illinois 60201

Cover and illustrations by Donna Currier
Book design by Rivera Design & Communications

ISBN # 0-9636187-1-7
Library of Congress Catalog Card Number: 95-94118

Printed in the United States of America

To my first hiking companions—
my husband and my children

PETER, NATHAN, AND MARGOT

Acknowledgments

I wish to express deep appreciation to my husband Peter who generously took time from his many university and research park duties to listen, to counsel, to wrestle with technical problems, and to offer editorial advice throughout this project.

I am profoundly indebted to Richard J. Kolecki, Superintendent of the Glenwood Hatchery, Colorado Division of Wildlife, who tutored me by telephone, by letter and in person about the raising of fish and the stocking of waters in northwest Colorado. His selfless participation allowed this fishing neophyte to get her feet wet.

To Larry D. Fredrick, dedicated volunteer researcher and lecturer at the Aspen Historical Society, I owe gratitude for his willingness to meet with me and to review portions of my manuscript in my attempt to accurately represent Aspen's past.

And I thank the many who patiently answered my questions, furnished new perspectives or responded to pages of my draft.

Edwin Allen, Superintendent, Rifle Falls Hatchery, Colorado DOW • John and Betsy Andersen, Parents & Hikers, Evanston, Ilinois • Fritz Benedict, Founder, 10th Mountain Division Hut System & Architect, FAIA • Jeffrey Bier, Broker, Mason and Morse Real Estate, Redstone • Chris Conrad, Assistant Town Planner, Snowmass Village • Douglas Dotson, Town Planner, Snowmass Village • Mark Fuller, Director of Open Space, Pitkin County • Allan Grimshaw, Lands and Minerals Officer, USFS • Robert Jacobson, Fishing Guide & Retail Sales Manager, Taylor Creek Guide Service • Ramona Markalunas, Aspen Historian • John McCarty, Landscape Architect & Environmental Planner, Snowmass Village • Gracie Oliphant, Naturalist, Snowmass Village • Douglass Purcell, Wildlife Technician, Crystal River Hatchery, Colorado DOW • John Riger, Superintendent, Crystal River Hatchery, Colorado DOW • Clee Sealing, Senior Fish Biologist, Colorado DOW • Samuel C. Schroeder, Forester & Fire Managment Officer, USFS • Walter C. Wieben, Rancher, Capitol Creek Valley.

Contents

Destinations

* Consult the chart on pages 187 and 188 for a complete listing of creeks, lakes, rivers, reservoirs and the fish that inhabit those waters.

REGIONAL OVERVIEW

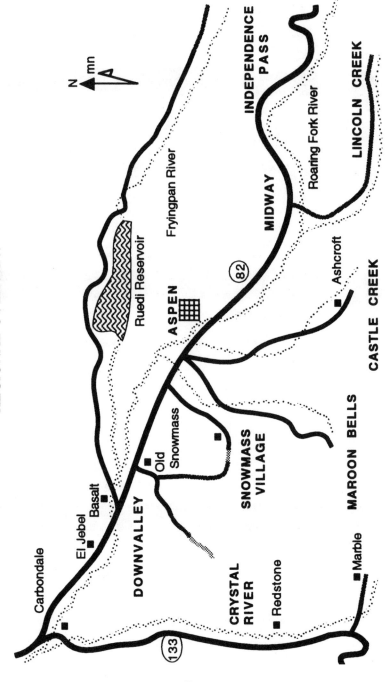

N mn

Carbondale

El Jebel

Basalt

Ruedi Reservoir

Fryingpan River

Old Snowmass

DOWNVALLEY

SNOWMASS VILLAGE

ASPEN

82

MIDWAY

INDEPENDENCE PASS

Roaring Fork River

LINCOLN CREEK

Ashcroft

CASTLE CREEK

MAROON BELLS

CRYSTAL RIVER

Redstone

133

Marble

Key to Icons

Hike Level of Difficulty

 Five hikes. Easiest excursions. Round trip distance of 1.0 to 3.8 miles. Maximum elevation gain of 240 feet. High point under 10,000 feet.

 Four hikes. Round trip distance of 1.8 to 4.6 miles. Elevation gain of 450 to 480 feet. High point under 10,000 feet.

 Eight hikes, six at high elevation. Round trip distance of 1.3 to 5.5 miles. Elevation gain of 493 to 1100 feet. High point of 8160 to 12,490 feet.

 Three hikes. Steady climbs. Round trip distance of 2.4 to 4.8 miles. Elevation gain of 1500 to 1700 feet. High point of 9400 to 12,000 feet.

Hike and Map Information

 Cold conditions possible. Warm clothing recommended.

 Marshy trail possible. Spare socks recommended.

 Minor stream crossing. Water flow variable. Spare socks.

 Four-wheel-drive necessary to reach hike's trailhead.

 Nature trail

 Fishing locale

 Ghost town

 Hike trailhead

Preface

Aspen and its incomparable outdoors are best explored on foot. For it is in unhurried moments that we begin to take the measure of a place—to hear its heartbeat, to touch its past, to sense its natural rhythms. **Aspen On Foot** helps visitors to experience uncommon places through walks across town and tundra. It was created to satisfy requests for trips less demanding than those featured in **The Aspen Dayhiker**, 1993. This new companion volume is designed for families, for novice mountaineers and for people with interests beyond the trail itself.

This guide introduces newcomers to the history of local hamlets, to the pleasures of mountain trails, to waters lively with trout, to winsome animals and to wildflower folklore. Its organization invites individuals and families to immerse themselves deeply into Aspen and into any of eight neighboring geographical regions. Each region has its own hikes and fishing spots plus a nature trail, ghost town, scenic lookout or village. A mammal and a plant found there are described and illustrated, and curious facts are tucked into each chapter.

Organization by region allows travelers with limited time to thoroughly investigate a territory, sampling contributions of both nature and man. Parents with young children know that a day of varied activities keeps everyone chipper. And visitors captivated by a particular locale can move on to more challenging trails in the **Dayhiker** or to books in this guide's bibliography.

The outdoor excursions are designed for people of all ages and fitness levels. Nature trails and the easiest hikes accommodate little children and languid walkers. Physical types can find several workout trails with major elevation gains. Minihikes range from one to five miles round trip; they include a paved riverside path, woodsy dirt tracks, and marshy byways over undulating tundra. Each hike write-up displays icons for difficulty rating and route characteristics. There is someplace for everyone—amateur naturalist, fisherman, photographer or power-walker.

Before you embark upon an adventure on foot, read "Mountain Hiking: The Basics." This preliminary chapter contains information to heighten your enjoyment and to keep you safe as you wander Colorado's exquisite mountains and valleys. Your experience may connect you to John Muir who wrote, "I only went out for a walk, and finally concluded to stay out till sundown, for going out, I found, was really going in."

Ruth Fredericks Frey

March 1995

"Walking is the best possible exercise."

—THOMAS JEFFERSON

MOUNTAIN HIKING
THE BASICS

WELLER LA

High Altitude
Hazards
Preparation
Trail Basics
Hiking with Children
Interpreting Hike Descriptions

"I went into the woods because I wished to live deliberately, to front only the essential facts of life, and see if I could not learn what it had to teach."

— HENRY DAVID THOREAU

High Altitude
How to Cope with Its Effects

YOU HAVE REALIZED YOUR PLANS FOR A MOUNTAIN VACATION, FLYING FROM A coastal city to Aspen, situated at 7908 feet of elevation. You are in good physical condition and eager to hike or bike. But you don't feel like yourself. Could this headache and fatigue signal the onset of flu? And why the heavy breathing after one flight of stairs? What is going on?

You are suffering the symptoms of mild mountain sickness as your body struggles to make the physiological changes necessary for normal functioning at high altitude. As you advance from low to high elevation, the air pressure drops. While the percentage of oxygen is the same in the mountains, the pressure driving it into your lungs, and thereby into your blood, is reduced. Your body responds by speeding up your breathing and raising your heart rate and blood pressure. This condition, called hypoxia, involves numerous chemical changes as well. In Aspen and Snowmass Village, each breath takes in only 70 to 80 percent of the oxygen available at sea level. No wonder you feel out of balance.

If you are susceptible to mountain sickness, you are most likely to feel your worst on the second or third day of your visit. The effects of high altitude diminish steadily thereafter, with the body making major adjustments in the first week and subtle adjustments for weeks to come.

And while other annoying problems are possible—insomnia, nausea, nasal congestion or constipation—the good news is that 75 percent of visitors adapt easily, experiencing only one or two symptoms. Some simple strategies can make everyone more comfortable.

Drink water. Several quarts of water or decaffeinated fluids per day are essential for fighting dehydration. Dry mountain air evaporates moisture more quickly from your body. This is aggravated by the intense sunlight and by exercise. Frequent urination results in more fluid loss as your kidneys work hard to thicken your blood. Drink often in town and on the trail. Do so even if you are not thirsty.

Avoid alcohol. Alcohol stimulates your kidneys, intensifying dehydration and retarding your adjustment to high elevation. And alcohol's effects at high altitude can be very much like those of a bad bout of mountain sickness. If you want to be active, be abstinent.

Don't overexercise. Increase physical activity gradually. Too much too soon could result in a combination of nasty symptoms. Start with trails such as the Rio Grande, Hunter Valley, Castle Creek, Avalanche Creek, Ditch or Wildcat Rim. Then move on to trips at higher elevations, such as those in the Maroon Bells, Midway or Independence Pass regions.

Eat lightly. Focus on carbohydrate foods: pasta, breads, potatoes, rice, fruits and vegetables. Carbohydrates require less oxygen for digestion than do fats and protein. They are also the best fuel for active endeavors.

Sleep. Plenty of rest will hasten acclimation and lessen the symptoms of mild mountain sickness, making you ready for more excursions among the splendid peaks and valleys of the Elk Mountains.

Your fingers look like plump sausages. They refuse instructions to undo buttons or tie shoelaces. Your rings will not budge. This is strange and a bit worrisome, but it is common among hikers. **Peripheral edema** is a painless swelling of the body's extremities caused by fluid retention or abnormal fluid distribution. Swelling of the hands, the least serious manifestation of edema, is usually caused by the dangling, swinging action of the arms, by compression from backpack straps, or by cold or heat. If you notice your hands beginning to swell, remove rings to prevent blood loss to fingers. And relax. Hands will return to normal a few hours after exercising.

Hazards
What to Avoid

THE EXCEPTIONAL BEAUTY OF THE ASPEN AREA MAKES MANY VISITORS FEEL they have been transported into a picture postcard. Crystalline streams sparkle with sunlight, billowy clouds caress mountaintops, snowfields irrigate flowery meadows. It looks idyllic and benign.

While veteran hikers savor these seductive images, they recognize in them some hidden hazards. That glorious sunshine can cause a wicked **sunburn**. At high elevation, strong ultraviolet light damages skin in any season. Don a hat and lather on sunscreen with a high SPF. And those crystalline streams harbor a microorganism introduced by mammalian feces. This intestinal parasite, **giardia lamblia**, causes severe cramps, bloating and diarrhea in infected humans. Symptoms appear up to two weeks after ingesting contaminated water. Even with medication, giardia can be hard to defeat. Never drink untreated water; always carry your liquids with you.

Swollen white puffs in a perfect blue heaven are picturesque as they waft above peaks. But in the mountains, especially on summer afternoons, those clouds can quickly mass into a dark, threatening ceiling. Rain may fall on Aspen's streets, but in the high country, hail batters the wildflowers and snow mantles the peaks. The wind rises and the temperature plummets. **Lightning** dances over the tundra, indiscriminate in its choice of targets. If you hike in alpine regions, watch the sky. When clouds begin to darken, turn back. Try to reach woods or your vehicle before the storm matures. The trails to Midway Pond and Linkins, Independence, Anderson and Lyle Lakes travel above treeline. The Wildcat Rim is an exposed ridge. Start these hikes in the morning, carry rain gear and stay alert.

Gorged with snowmelt in early summer, mountain creeks are swift, frigid and deep. Beneath the **turbulent water** are round, slick stones. Should your trail approach such a tumult, restrain young children and do not attempt a ford. Water flow will diminish weekly, making a safe crossing probable in the future. Lingering snow can camouflage depressions, overhang trails and conceal tunnels of rushing snowmelt. Choose to detour around major **snowfields**.

The discomforts of mild mountain sickness can intensify with an increase in altitude and exertion. A walk on the flat Rio Grande Trail at 7900 feet will stress your body less than a 1500 foot climb to Midway Pond's height of 12,000 feet. In some individuals the extra demands of an uphill hike at a higher elevation can result in **acute mountain sickness**. Its symptoms include severe headache, nausea, vomiting, lethargy, breathlessness at rest, loss of coordination and judgment, reduced urine output and facial swelling. Do not ignore these signs. They can develop into grave illnesses. Descend to lower elevation. Drink liberal quantities of fluid. Rest. Seek medical help if the problems persist or worsen.

Avoid Problems

Apply a sunscreen

Carry all drinking water

Monitor the sky

Shun swollen creeks

Bypass deep snow

Descend if ill

Stay dry and warm

This guide features short introductory hikes rather than extended treks deep into wilderness areas. While the risk of **hypothermia** is much greater on more ambitious trips, all hikers must recognize the conditions contributing to this potentially fatal illness. Hypothermia is a dangerous decrease in the temperature of the body's vital inner core. It can begin when wetness from a rainstorm, from a tumble into a creek, or from heavy perspiration is combined with a cold and windy day. Fatigue is a major factor. The mix can be a lethal if the victim remains wet, exposed and tired. Violent shivering, stumbling, slowed speech, exhaustion and incoherence are the first signs of trouble. Do not wait for symptoms to appear. Find shelter from the wind or rain. Replace wet clothing with dry garments. Cover head, neck and hands. Insulate the victim from snow and cold rocks. Offer food and warm liquids if possible. Keep the victim awake. Better yet, never attempt lengthy excursions or tundra hikes without rain gear, extra clothing and plentiful snacks for delivery of energy and heat.

Preparation
Where to Start and What to Carry

A MAJORITY OF THE TRAILS DESCRIBED IN THIS GUIDE STAY BELOW $10,000$ feet of elevation. Of these, only the Sunnyside and Ute hikes are strenuous climbs. The remaining trips under $10,000$ feet are fine introductions for newcomers to the mountains; they accommodate families with children, hikers with limited time, and visitors with average levels of fitness; and journeys at moderate elevation are excellent warm-ups for people interested in more ambitious treks above treeline. Read hike descriptions and then choose from these walks for your initial excursions.

Starting gradually allows everyone to acclimate to altitude and reduces anxiety in the uninitiated. It also uncovers problems with footgear, equipment, mental attitude or physical conditioning that could jeopardize future hikes. It is important not to overestimate the interest, stamina and speed of your hiking companions: Consider the least able participant and the trail's level of difficulty when selecting your first outing. You will quickly learn what is appropriate.

Planning should include the time of departure. An early morning start is essential for all hikes that traverse alpine areas and for all hikes that originate far from a town. Afternoon thunderstorms and muddy, slick 4WD roads are real hazards. For dayhikes within wooded areas or close to civilization, the hour of departure is less critical. If you are tempted by the description of a major hike extension, pack your gear the night before and rise early.

The items essential for a successful short dayhike are few: good shoes, drinking water, sunscreen and a waterproof jacket. Beyond the easiest jaunts, additional supplies are recommended. And for extended hikes and those above treeline, more gear is necessary. Supplies fall into three

Wise Decisions

Read trail descriptions

Begin with easier hikes

Consider abilities of companions

Rise early for certain trips

7

general categories: covering for your body, food for your belly and stuff for your pack.

Consider your feet first. Comfortable, supportive shoes are crucial to your enjoyment of the outdoors. Minihikes require less serious footgear than backpack trips or marathon dayhikes. Running shoes, featherweight hiking boots or one of the new hybrids will suffice. A deeply textured sole is very helpful on steep inclines, gravelly surfaces and slippery rocks. And while any hightop athletic shoe provides some ankle support and protection from rocks, go with what feels right. It is important that your toes should not touch the front of your shoe or boot and that your heel should not slip when the shoe is laced.

Socks should be appropriate for your shoe. Fit is everything. Acrylic, polypropylene and wool are recommended over cotton which traps heat and fails to wick moisture away from skin. Thicker socks provide some cushioning. Carry a spare pair of socks if your chosen trail crosses a creek or marshland. Those spares can always double as mittens on a cold day.

Dress for Success

Select shoes carefully

Fit socks to shoes

Layer your clothing

Prepare for sun, rain and cold

A layered approach to clothing is best in the mountains where temperatures vary widely. A tee shirt worn under a fleece pullover, wool sweater or heavy shirt will do for chilly mornings or walks across tundra. A hooded wind-rain jacket is an essential outer layer for cold or wet conditions. Shorts or lightweight trousers go everywhere; rain pants are good insurance for lengthy, high-altitude treks. A brimmed hat and tinted glasses with UV protection guard against sun, while a warm cap and mittens are often needed in alpine regions such as Independence Pass.

Trail food is fun food. It keeps children happy and keeps everyone energized. Hiking justifies snacking. Nibbling often on carbohydrate foods is the standard strategy for refueling while exercising. A short walk might require only a few morsels for children; a journey of a half-day or more can include a variety of goodies and substantial lunch foods. A backpack becomes a portable pantry and something of a security blanket.

But not all snacks are good snacks. On longer hikes, go easy on foods heavily laden with fat and sugar. The fat content of peanut butter, cheeses and processed meats works against hikers: Fats contribute to lethargy; they are slow to digest and slow to convert to energy. An excess of sugar produces power surges followed by fatigue as blood sugar levels rise and fall. While gorp is a favorite trail food, its creative mix of nuts, dried fruits and coated chocolate bits delivers fat and sugar and requires extra water for digestion. All this is fine—in moderation.

Carbohydrate foods are just right: They digest easily and soon replenish exhausted energy stores. Fresh apples, oranges, grapes, cherries and veggie sticks travel well. So do bagels, dense fruit-nut breads, English muffins, pretzels and rice cakes. Lowfat sports bars, cookies and crackers are good, but do read labels on these and other prepared snacks. Consider dry cereals, cold pasta or pita bread stuffed with vegetables. Be imaginative. Reusable, zip-top bags are wonderful containers for everything, including ripe raspberries or serviceberries discovered along your route.

All mountain walks, short or long, require water. Intense sunshine, parched air and moisture lost through perspiration contribute to dehydration and to the serious problems of heat exhaustion, heat stroke and mountain sickness. The best strategy is to drink frequently and before you are thirsty; the desire for liquid usually follows the onset of dehydration. Water is absorbed quickly and is fine for most hikes. Diluted juices may appeal to some children, and cold, flavored herb teas may be the choice of some adults. Should you decide to tackle a long hike, consider trying one of the many sports drinks available. They hydrate while increasing endurance with their combination of simple carbohydrate sugars, electrolytes and glucose polymers. Always carry more fluids than you expect to need.

Fuel Your Body

Snack often for energy

Pack carbohydrate foods

Go easy on fat and sugar

Drink at regular intervals

Carry extra water

Basic gear for a minihike of a mile or two may be little more than a **water bottle** worn at the waist and a few small items tucked into a pocket. A fanny pack with

9

attached water bottles is usually enough for a half-day trip. But for a longer journey, or if hiking with children, be well prepared. While each hiker can carry **personal provisions**—drinking water, a whistle, a jacket, spare socks, lip balm, an energy bar, prescription medicine—at least one member of the group should wear a **backpack** large enough to contain an assortment of useful things.

For the designated carrier(s), the following **small supplies** are suggested:

- sunscreen
- mosquito repellent
- moleskin for blisters
- pocketknife with a scissor tool
- sealed, moist towelettes for scrapes
- breathable tape for hot spots
- bandages of varying sizes
- antibiotic first aid cream
- aspirin or ibuprofen
- bandana for sling, tourniquet, etc.
- safety pins
- tweezers for slivers, thorns, ticks
- guidebook or map
- bag for trash

Fun **extras** include a camera, binoculars, a nature field guide, a magnifying lens and fishing gear. Lengthy challenging hikes are beyond the scope of this book. But if you are planning a major trip, additional essentials include a lighter or waterproof matches, a compass, a flashlight, tablets for water purification, an insulating clothing layer, rain pants and a heat-reflective body bag or blanket.

Trail Basics
What Seasoned Hikers Know

I F YOU ARE NEW TO MOUNTAIN PATHS, YOUR UNDERSTANDING OF SUBTLE ROUTE markings, trail etiquette and safety rules will help you hike like a veteran. Staying alert and aware of surroundings will almost guarantee a good trip.

Counsel comes in many forms: guidebooks, regional and topographical maps, trail and wilderness boundary signs, trailhead register boxes and advice from personnel at mountaineering stores. Reading, watching for markers and listening to experienced hikers is often enough for a successful excursion. But sometimes additional observational skills are needed to get you to your destination and back.

Before you step over those logs or branches lying across the trail, look at them again. Are they deadfall, casually tumbled to earth? Or are they trees cut with a saw and placed in your way? These obstacles could signal a closed route or a dead-end spur. The main trail is likely to be nearby, angling off in another direction.

If you encounter no fallen trees to halt your progress but notice the path fading beneath your feet, you have probably missed a turn and are following an animal trail or an eroded strip of ground. Retrace your steps to discover the primary route.

Subtle Markers
Fallen trees
Faint paths
Cairns

Across open spaces—boulderfields and tundra—the most common markers are small piles of rocks called cairns. They can be subtle indeed, blending perfectly with the natural surroundings. Scan the terrain carefully to locate a cairn and walk from one to the next. Cairns have been constructed by hikers and by the Forest Service. Sometimes they need repair. Add a rock or two.

11

Hikers seek something special from the outdoors, something that cannot be obtained from everyday experiences at work, at school, at home. Observing trail etiquette maximizes everyone's pleasure. It is good for the environment, for fellow travelers and for you.

High elevation, a short growing season, extremes of weather and a dearth of moisture combine in the mountains, creating unique and fragile vegetation. Stay on the designated trail to protect what takes so long to mature. And leave all flowers for others to admire. Some are protected by law; others will not reproduce if picked.

Always carry away all that you have brought with you. Leave no trace of your passing—no paper, no eggshells, no orange peels, nothing. Do not foul this beautiful land. And when looking for a place to urinate, move 200 feet from a lake or creek. Wild water needs protection too.

Should other hikers overtake your group, stand aside to let them pass. They may have a long journey requiring a faster pace. The horses you encounter have the right of way. As a horse could become agitated in your presence, move calmly off the trail to prevent injury to yourself or to the hapless rider. Dogs accompany some hikers, and, if running free, can frighten people, horses and wildlife. The law requires that dogs be leashed within wilderness areas. If you must bring your pet, show respect for the other living beings you meet.

Finally, imitate the quiet ways of Native Americans and wild creatures. Lowered voices, whispers and silence preserve a sense of wilderness and allow you to view mammals and birds in their natural habitats. And a hushed voice befits outdoor temples built of ancient stones and evergreen columns.

Mountain exploration is exhilarating, and with adherence to a few basic rules, it can be safe as well. While the trails described in this guide are relatively short, well-traveled and well-marked,

Trail Etiquette

Stay on the trail

Do not pick flowers

Never litter

Let faster hikers pass

Give horses the right of way

Leash your dog

Maintain a quiet presence

a few traverse alpine tundra or lie far from towns. Many trails have tempting extensions. These trips should not be undertaken carelessly.

Safe Conduct

Learn about your route

Tell someone where you are going

Sign in at the trailhead

Stay with companions

Carry a whistle

Stay put if lost

Before departing, learn about your route and pack a map and a compass. Always tell a non-hiker where you are going and when you expect to be back. Then sign in at the trailhead registration box. If you do not return, the Forest Service or Mountain Rescue can verify your whereabouts, giving focus and speed to a search.

Practice the buddy system. Do not hike solo, do not speed ahead of the group, and do not leave a slower companion behind once the trip is underway. Stick together. Accidents, sickness, sudden storms, hypothermia and indistinct trails should not be faced alone.

Carry a whistle and suggest that fellow hikers add them to their pockets. Three blasts on a whistle is an international distress signal. It carries farther than your voice and should be employed only in an emergency. If you are hurt and alone, use your whistle. And should you become hopelessly lost, step away from a noisy creek, blow on your whistle and stop wandering. Searchers cover ground in an organized fashion. If you continue to move, you may enter an area already searched and scratched from the schedule.

Numbers to Know

Emergency/Mt. Rescue 911

U.S. Forest Service-Aspen 925-3445

Aspen Valley Hospital 925-1120

Hiking With Children
How to Have a Happy and Safe Expedition

HIKING IS AN IDEAL FAMILY ACTIVITY AS IT IS EASY TO LEARN AND INEXPENSIVE to practice. The nature trails in this guide are good preliminary excursions for the youngest children, while many of the hiking trails are suitable for those age six and older. A successful trip is likely if the trail is selected to match the children's abilities and if the adults in the group are sensitive to the children's interests and safety. There are simple strategies for a happy ramble in the mountains.

Be positive. Your own enthusiasm is contagious. After choosing a hike, talk about the destination and the things expected along the trail. Use words like "explore," "discover" and "adventure" to pique young imaginations. Reassure them that this is a "walk" and that there will be pauses to scout for animal tracks, to listen to aspen trees, to smell evergreen needles or to watch fishermen casting lines into creeks.

Assign responsibility. Even the youngest hiker can carry a plastic water bottle in a holster belt or an energy bar in a pocket. Older children can wear small daypacks holding water, a snack and a rain jacket. Including children in the planning process and assigning them care of essential supplies creates a team feeling, making everyone feel important.

Share leadership. Allow each child to "lead" for a designated number of minutes or to a designated landmark along the trail. Short stints can build confidence. But stay close to your young pathfinder and firmly outlaw any running ahead of the group.

Offer praise. Verbal rewards—especially those given in the presence of other hikers—will move you along. Positive reinforcement works. Start praising children early in the trek.

Be patient. Allow extra time when hiking with children. They care less about the destination than about the little surprises and curiosities encountered along the way. If you really want to reach a specific goal at a specific pace, plan to do it alone.

Provide snacks. An ample supply of trail food accomplishes two important goals: It refuels little bodies with energy, and it rewards young hikers for their new accomplishments. Provide snacks at regular intervals to maintain energy levels and promise a favorite treat for reaching that hilltop, pond or meadow ahead. Call it bribery, if you like. Food is a powerful motivator.

Play games. Creative entertainment sustains children's interest. A search for things fuzzy, prickly, slippery, sticky and rough lets them explore with their hands. Their noses can sniff out the most fragrant flower and tree. Practice walking silently like coyotes and Native American hunters or try to advance from stepstone to stepstone. Counting games can focus on colors in nature or footprints on the trail. Sticks are multipurpose resources: Forage for the perfect walking staffs; fasten bandanas to sticks to make family banners; launch twig boats on streams to learn about water flow.

Celebrate achievement. Reaching a carefully chosen destination is an opportunity for a family picnic and a time to let children explore nearby on their own. Granting them a bit of freedom revives spirits. Be watchful but not intrusive. You may be amazed by the energy displayed by "worn out" hikers.

While keeping children cheerful on the trail is nice, keeping them safe is paramount. The high altitude environment and the wild, unfamiliar terrain require special vigilance from parents. **Carry first aid supplies** and be sympathetic to the smallest "injuries." Remember that children are comforted by band-aids.

Monitor fluids. Adults and children who exercise at high elevation should take frequent water breaks to avoid dehydration and mountain sickness. Pause briefly every 15 or 20 minutes to drink. Carefully monitor each child's fluid intake, asking that he or she sip some water or juice even if not thirsty. This is a good time to explain that creek and lake water is unsafe to drink because of a tiny parasite called giardia.

Be observant. Listen to children's complaints and watch their behavior. Fatigue could be simple weariness or a symptom of mountain sickness. An upset stomach, headache, dizziness or loss of coordination likely signals a bad response to high elevation. Shivering, listlessness, stumbling or slurred speech on a damp, windy day suggests hypothermia; children are particularly susceptible but may deny feeling cold. Be ready to turn back if your child's behavior changes. The trail will be there tomorrow.

Teach safety. Tell your children to stay close to you on the trail, explaining that wild places have unfamiliar dangers. Instruct them to remain in one place if they do become separated from the group; tell them that they will be found more quickly if they do not wander about. Present each child with a whistle to wear or carry. Explain that it must be used only in an emergency, such as becoming lost, and that three blasts of the whistle is a recognized call for help.

Interpreting Hike Descriptions
How to Choose a Trail

WHEN REALITY CONFORMS TO EXPECTATIONS, PLEASURE AND COMFORT ARE maximized. You have sought out a mountain experience. Make it wonderful by anticipating each outdoor adventure realistically.

Every minihike description in this guide begins with a summary of trail characteristics. Start your assessment here, keeping in mind the capabilities and concerns of all companions, the number of days at high altitude, and the hours you can allot to a hike. If the trailhead lies many miles from your lodging, for example, factor in the extra driving time.

The expressive face icon on page one of each minihike write-up symbolizes the level of difficulty *relative to other hikes in this guide*. It does not represent a standard used statewide, or even locally, to rate difficulty. It may be helpful to know, however, that the most challenging trips in **Aspen On Foot** correspond to the easiest trips in **The Aspen Dayhiker**, a companion guide from Brush Creek Books. A global assessment of difficulty is obviously personal and subjective, but the icons do indicate that one trip is slightly or significantly harder than another. Your own exertion will reveal how much difference separates the rankings.

Note that the trail summary does not include an estimate of hiking time. This is hiking's greatest variable, subject to motivation and fitness and to individual preferences for bird-watching, photography, rest stops and side trips. On dayhikes venturing far into wilderness areas, a snappy pace and brief pauses are the rule. The minihikes featured here place no such requirements on walkers. These short rambles allow ample time for a leisurely tempo, for nature study and for trout fishing. Relax and savor the summertime beauty of the mountains. Just remember to rise early for tundra walks to avoid an afternoon scramble for shelter.

Hiking Distance in miles is provided for each trip; it is followed by Elevation Gain in feet. *They must be considered together.* A four-mile walk on level ground is generally easier than a two-mile march over rolling up and down terrain: The variance between the Rio Grande and the Wildcat Rim trails is a good example. A short distance paired with a large elevation gain indicates considerable steepness and is usually rated as most difficult: The Ute and Sunnyside trails fall in this category. And always check the hike's High Point. Any trail that travels at an elevation over 10,000 feet is more taxing due to the thin air.

The Highlights, the Fishing and the Nearby Attractions notations, plus the Comments paragraph, may help you make a final decision. The book's arrangement by geographical regions allows visitors to pair a half-day walk with a stop for fishing or a visit to a nature trail, ghost town, viewspot or local village.

Use Trail Summary

Check overall difficulty rating

Assess companions' abilities

Factor in time and interests

Note distance relative to elevation gain

Consider altitude of hike

Choose nearby excursions

ASPEN

ASPEN REGION

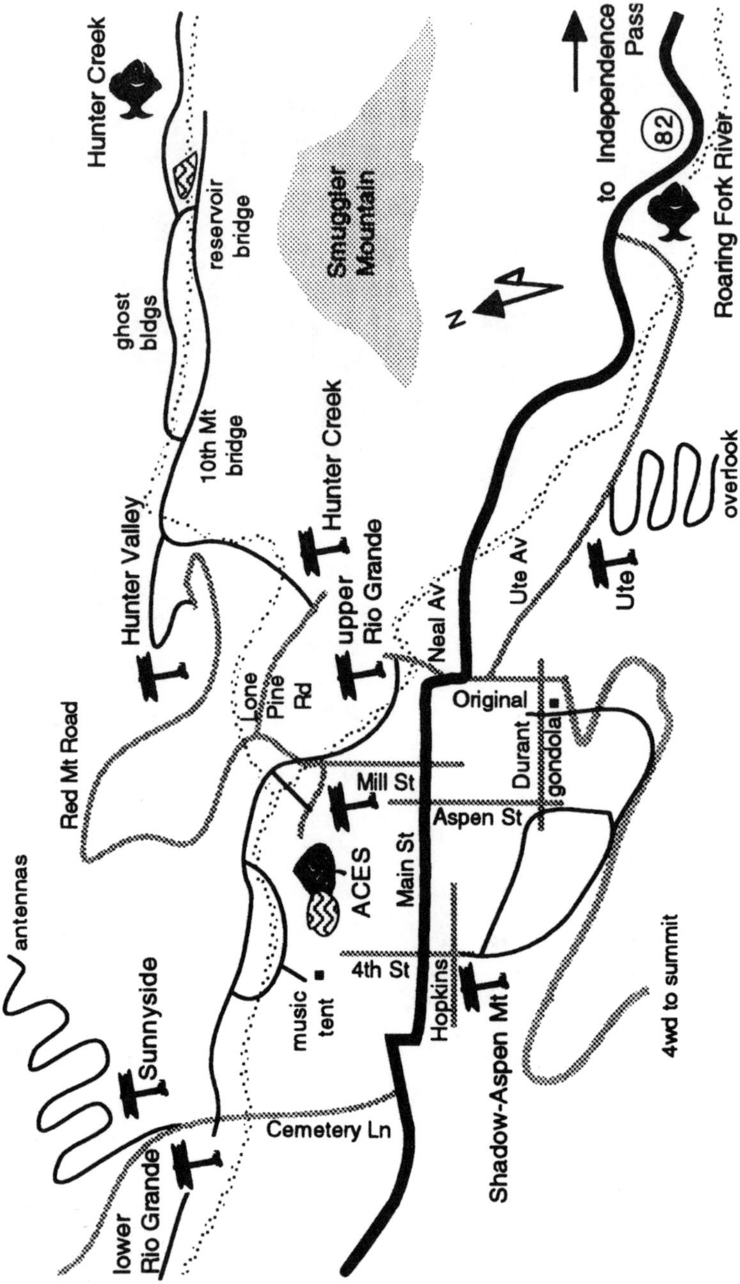

Hunter Creek

ghost bldgs

reservoir bridge

Smuggler Mountain

to Independence Pass

Roaring Fork River

82

N

10th Mt bridge

Hunter Valley

Hunter Creek

upper Rio Grande

Red Mt Road

Lone Pine Rd

Neal Av.

Ute Av.

Ute

overlook

antennas

Sunnyside

ACES

Mill St

Aspen St

Original

Durant

gondola

Main St

music tent

4th St

Hopkins

Shadow-Aspen Mt

4wd to summit

Cemetery Ln

lower Rio Grande

Old Aspen
The Silver Years

GEOLOGICAL SURVEYS OF THE EARLY 1870s SUGGESTED MINERAL WEALTH IN the Roaring Fork Valley. So when the rugged land between Leadville and the Continental Divide was ceded to whites by the Ute Indians in 1878, prospectors and speculators headed west, undeterred by the lofty mountains, winter avalanches, summer storms, isolation, renegade natives and the financial perils of their profession. In the summer of 1879 gold was found near the Divide, giving birth to the Independence mining camp. The first silver claims were staked out in the pretty Roaring Fork Valley 20 miles farther west.

Late in the year entrepreneur Henry Gillespie tromped into that valley with some miners from Leadville. The group had crossed the Divide in record time by traveling only at night when the snow was hard enough to support them and their steel-bottomed, wooden supply "boats." Gillespie had plans to plat the town and build a road to Buena Vista. He organized the camp residents and quickly headed east to raise money and secure a post office to validate the place he called Ute City. But B. Clark Wheeler, teacher, lawyer and promoter, was ambitious too. In February of 1880 he arrived from Leadville. He surveyed the land and laid out streets, naming them for town pioneers and for the eastern capitalists who were his fellow investors: Gillespie, Hallam, Hyman, Cooper, Hopkins and Deane. He named his creation Aspen and gave it legal status. Almost overnight, in tents and rustic log cabins, people were in business. Aspen soon had its first hotel, restaurant, assay and law offices, survey and engineering firms, sawmill and saloon.

Both Gillespie and Wheeler made early investments but were especially significant in promoting a town that would be legendary. By late 1880 Gillespie had his toll road to Buena Vista via Taylor Pass from the Ashcroft mining camp in Castle Creek Valley. B. Clark Wheeler's toll road over Independence Pass to Leadville was completed the next year. But both routes were obstructed by rocks, potholes and tree stumps and were impassable from deep snow and mud much of the time. Aspen remained isolated, far from a railroad and without an efficient means to transport ore over the surrounding mountains. Until 1883, mining in Aspen was minimal, limited primarily to exploration, claim jumping and litigation over ownership.

Nonetheless, the handful of optimistic year-round residents, led by Mrs. Henry Gillespie, founded a literary society, held concerts and dances, began a Sabbath school and established a Ladies Aid Society. Citizens later planted trees to beautify their town and organized a baseball team. In February of 1881 their application for county status was approved, establishing Pitkin County. In May, Aspen held its first municipal elections. The fledgling *Aspen Times* and the *Rocky Mountain Sun* newspapers began promoting the settlement, and the Corkhill Opera House opened by year's end.

While the 1882 arrival of telegraph service connected Aspen's people to the outside world, Aspen's riches went nowhere until wealthy Easterner Jerome B. Wheeler was persuaded to visit the town in 1883. This partner in R.H. Macy & Company of New York saw Aspen's potential and its dire need for both a smelter to process ore and a railroad to transport it from the valley. He spent money quickly for mines and for an unfinished smelter on Castle Creek. He opened a bank and constructed roads. Within a year Aspen's silver production rose from nothing to five tons of concentrate a day.

A major fire in Aspen's downtown in 1884 spurred two major mine owners and town pioneers to develop the Aspen Water Company. Thanks to David R.C. Brown and Henry P. Cowenhoven, water flowed into town from reservoirs near Castle and Maroon Creeks in 1886. And to meet another need, the Roaring Fork Power Company built the nation's first commercially operated hydroelectric plant. The growing male population had lusty appetites, consuming enormous quantities of beer, prompting construction of a brewery. The men also frequented Aspen's "sporting houses," which prospered in the Durant Street red light district. The miners were keen on gambling, boxing, horse racing and baseball, diversions from one of the world's most hazardous occupations. A new roller rink and theatre offered more genteel entertainments.

With the arrival of two railroads—the Denver & Rio Grande in 1887 and the Colorado Midland in 1888—Aspen's silver production and population rose sharply, and the town acquired many impressive brick and sandstone buildings. Jerome Wheeler built the fine Wheeler Opera House and the luxurious Jerome Hotel in 1889. Social and cultural events became more sophisticated and even attracted European visitors. Three dailies and three weeklies published news. A substantial brick hospital was built with funds contributed by the citizenry. By 1892 Aspen claimed about 11,000 permanent residents, twice its population a century later. Pitkin County's developed mines totalled over 200 and employed about 2500 miners earning three dollars a day. The productive Mollie Gibson and Smuggler were among the richest silver mines in the world.

But there was a downside to this newly industrialized city. The mining, processing and transporting of ore seriously fouled the air and water; noise was unrelenting; hillsides were stripped of trees needed for construction and fuel. Environmentally induced illness were common. Hard rock miners were especially vulnerable, suffering from tuberculosis, pneumonia, typhoid, dysentery, giardia, rheumatism, alcoholism, drug addiction, venereal disease, malnutrition and injuries. Suicide claimed others. The pristine valley of the Utes was no more.

The 1893 Columbian Exhibition in Chicago displayed a glistening statue, the "Silver Queen," partially crafted from Aspen's ore. It was intended to revive the U.S. government's flagging interest in silver. But that was not to be. That same year the government abandoned the silver standard for gold with the repeal of the Sherman Silver Purchase Act. Even before silver's devaluation, many of

Aspen's mines had shut down. People abandoned homes and businesses. Though ghost towns appeared all over the west, Aspen, with its more stable institutions, continued to function as a community. Ironically, in 1894, the biggest silver nugget ever unearthed, possibly 2260 pounds, was pulled from the Smuggler Mine. Yet, despite a limited revival of mining, by 1900 Aspen's population had dropped to about 5,000; by 1930, only about 700 people remained in what had became a trading center for the valley's ranchers and potato farmers.

The Biking Craze

Bicycling on mountain roads seems contemporary, hip, new. But not so. In the late 1880s Aspen's men and women formed bicycle clubs, held competitions and built a quarter-mile bike track in cooperation with the baseball club—which needed help constructing its ball field. Men donned blazers embellished with club insignias, and women sported bloomers for ease in riding. As part of the rivalry with the Denver & Rio Grande Railroad, the Colorado Midland provided free excursion trains so that spectators could comfortably roll alongside bicycle races from Aspen to Basalt. Considering the state of roads and of bicycle technology in the 1880s, it is a wonder that any competitors crossed the finish line.

Aspen Reborn
The Renaissance

ALTHOUGH OVER A CENTURY SEPARATES ASPEN'S MINING HEYDAY FROM ITS supremacy today as a cultural and skiing mecca, some of the town's earliest residents had a prophetic vision. Committed to permanence and civilization, the 14 women who bravely remained for the winter of 1880-81 began instructive and social institutions that were to give Aspen a western sophistication unknown in most mining communities. Their husbands used leisure hours to explore the snowy terrain on skis, often just barrel staves, banded to their heavy boots.

The foundation was laid unknowingly for a future as glittering as the silvery past. The pioneers' choice of townsite amidst exquisite mountain beauty and the endurance of handsome structures, such as the Wheeler Opera House, the Hotel Jerome and the Pitkin County Courthouse, made Aspen a natural place for a twentieth century renaissance community—one dedicated to the outdoors, to learning and to the arts.

A meeting at the 1936 Olympics in Germany between two Americans, outdoorsman Ted Ryan and bobsled racer Billy Fiske, germinated the idea for a premium ski resort in the United States. Just weeks later Fiske was introduced to Thomas Flynn, an Aspen miner's son, who showed him a photograph of Aspen Mountain with hopes of selling some mining claims. Fiske was beguiled by the scenery. He toured the Aspen area, took an option on some land and told Ryan he had found their skiing paradise at Ashcroft's Hayden Peak. The two embarked on the project, building a lodge and hiring the Swiss mountaineer, engineer and skier Andre Roch to study the terrain. Locals, already enjoying winter sports, quickly appreciated the value of promoting their powdery snow.

Roch saw an exciting future for the Hayden Peak site but recommended starting with Aspen Mountain where a base village already stood. Plans went forward for Hayden while Roch designed a challenging run down Aspen Mountain, complete with corkscrew turns and a 2000 foot vertical drop. A new and enthusiastic local ski club and WPA crews cleared the steep terrain in the summer of 1937. Roch Run became the site for major races in 1939 and 1941.

But when Billy Fiske was killed in 1940 while fighting for England in World War II, Ryan stopped work at Ashcroft and leased the lodge to the U.S. Army 87th Mountain Infantry for winter training. When the 87th was integrated into the 10th Mountain Division at Camp Hale near Leadville, word of Aspen's good skiing attracted soldiers with weekend leaves. Captivated by the place, many 10th Mountaineers pledged to return after the war. Nearly 20 would do so.

In 1945 the first to arrive included ski instructor Friedl Pfeifer and architect Fritz Benedict. While serving in Italy, Pfeifer had dreamed of ski runs and Benedict of Red Mountain ranch land. The cultured, vibrant humanist Elizabeth Nitze Paepcke had returned as well, introducing her husband Walter, a Chicago industrialist and intellectual, to this place that had so impressed her on a visit six years earlier. Walter quickly understood her enchantment and recognized Aspen's promise. He presented an astonished Elizabeth with an old Victorian house as a birthday gift the day after their arrival. This deteriorating dwelling symbolized commitment.

An inspired Walter Paepcke assembled Aspen's citizens to expound upon his ambitious dream for the languid town. The audience was unimpressed. But Walter, undeterred by local public opinion, gave financial help to Pfeifer who wished to purchase mining claims to develop ski runs. The Paepckes brought Bauhaus architect Herbert Bayer to town to join the young Benedict; created The Aspen Company to buy property and renovate neglected Victorian buildings; and, with Pfeifer, Paul Nitze and others, formed the Aspen Skiing Corporation. Pfeifer began a ski school and was joined by Swiss skier Fred Iselin. By 1946 Aspen had the world's longest chair lift system, and in

1950 Aspen hosted America's first World Alpine Ski Championships, giving the young resort international status.

But Paepcke also intended Aspen to be "a community of peace with opportunities for a man's complete life... where he can earn a living, profit by healthy, physical recreation, with facilities at hand for his enjoyment of art, music, and education." His was the vision of the "Universal Man," and Aspen seemed the very place to realize the Greek ideal of the complete life. In this spirit, the Paepckes assembled luminaries Albert Schweitzer, Artur Rubenstein, Thornton Wilder, Dimitri Mitropoulos, Gregor Piatigorski, Jose Ortega y Gassett and other great minds and talents for celebration of the Goethe Bicentennial in 1949, an international event that inaugurated Aspen as an intellectual and cultural center. Here the Aspen Institute for Humanistic Studies, the Aspen Music Festival, the Aspen Music School and the International Design Conference were conceived.

But the Paepckes were not finished. They helped establish Aspen Airways, and after her husband's death in 1960, Elizabeth founded the Aspen Center for Environmental Studies, donating its beautiful acreage and adjacent land for the Given Biomedical Institute. The Aspen Center for Physics, an outgrowth of the Aspen Institute, was annexed to enduring institutions. With the addition of DanceAspen, art galleries, theatre, festivals and a plethora of outdoor sporting activities, summer sparkles today like winter snow.

And so it was that nineteenth century New Yorker Jerome Wheeler and twentieth century Chicagoans Elizabeth and Walter Paepcke gave life, prosperity and cultural institutions to a sleepy Colorado town. Many are grateful for their prescience.

Aspen Center for Environmental Studies

Tucked into a quiet hollow in Aspen only one block west of the post office is a wonderful resource for anyone with curiosity about the natural world. The 25-acre preserve at Hallam Lake is an ideal first stop for a close-up introduction to the ecology of the Elk Mountains. Visitors to the wildlife sanctuary and education center may take a self-guided nature tour on a loop trail bordering lake, marsh, meadow, beaver ponds and river; they may go on walks led by naturalists in four area locales; and they may attend varied presentations at specified hours. Parents may place children in programs lasting one hour to one day and may register themselves for adult Naturalist Field School classes lasting one to seven days.

The Aspen Center for Environmental Studies is a living museum for people of all ages. Even the youngest children can handle the nature trail, and they will be intrigued by the free-roaming wildlife, the Bird of Prey House and all orphaned and injured creatures tended by the ACES staff. A boardwalk allows wheelchair access to a small portion of the grounds. Binoculars and trail guides may be borrowed for your visit, and a small shop offers books for adults and children, hand lenses for study of tiny wonders, and assorted items related to the natural environment.

During Aspen's silver boom years in the late 1880s, Hallam Lake was a recreation center with an amusement park, dance pavilion and rental boats. A popular feature was a "tunnel of love" boat slide into the water. Ice cut from the lake in winter provided refrigeration for food year round. Aspen's population plummeted after the silver crash of 1893, and by the early 1900s the park's land was sold and utilized for grazing.

Elizabeth Paepcke, a founder of modern Aspen, purchased the lakeside acreage in the 1950s. In the late 1960s she donated the parcel for a wildlife

28

sanctuary and created ACES. In the next decade Stuart Mace, environmentalist and educator, helped ACES define its mission by teaching children to have empathy with nature so they might mature to serve as Earth's stewards. Thus, Hallam Lake plays a new role today as an outdoor laboratory—a place for the preservation and study of a special riparian ecology. A current project aims to create a breeding population of pure, A+ strain Colorado River cutthroat trout, a threatened native species.

Aspen to Destination: To visit ACES, head south two blocks on Mill Street from Main. At Puppy Smith Street turn left and walk past the market and post office to the street's end. A short and shady footpath leads to the education building and preserve. ACES is open Monday through Saturday. Call 925-5756 for additional information about nature walks and classes.

> *"The goal of all our programs remains educating people to be environmentally responsible."*
>
> —Elizabeth Paepke

Aspen Mountain and the Silver Queen Gondola

ASPEN MOUNTAIN, THE MIGHTY BACKDROP FOR THIS PICTURESQUE TOWN, IS strongly identified with winter skiing. Rightly so. But Aspen Mountain, bedecked in wildflowers and bustling with wild creatures, has a seductive summer beauty. Up close, vivid blossoms mingle on nature's verdant palette. From the summit, distant ranges are painted in muted hues. The mountain's native residents add a sense of man's connection to Earth's fellows. Right in Aspen's backyard, the mountain awaits visitors scouting for physical challenge, alpine scenery or a field study venue.

The mountain's peak is high, high above the town. Aspen's official elevation is 7908 feet; Aspen Mountain's base is measured at 7945 feet; and its summit is 11,212 feet above sea level. Gain access to the top by a 18-minute ride in the Silver Queen Gondola or by a stiff uphill hike.

Operated by the Aspen Skiing Company, the gondola operates daily from mid-June until early September and on spring and fall weekends before and after that daily service period. Uphill rides begin at 9:30 a.m. in summer; the final descent is at 4:30 p.m. Purchase tickets at the gondola's base terminal on Durant Street near the Little Nell Hotel. The trip down is free for anyone who reaches the mountain's peak on foot.

The Silver Queen was dedicated in January of 1987 and has an impressive vertical rise of 3267 feet. Each of the gondola's cabins transports six passengers to the mountain's summit where visitors can explore the terrain, dig out camera or binoculars, or settle in at the Sundeck restaurant. The Aspen Center for Environmental Studies conducts free, daily nature walks each summer. Excursions depart on the hour from 10:00 a.m. until 2:00 p.m. Weekly musical events and children's programs are also scheduled on this lofty stage. The panorama includes the nearby Highlands ski area, the peaks of the Elk Range, the Williams Mountains and the Sawatch Range. Remember that summit temperatures are much cooler than those in town.

The hike up Aspen Mountain is wonderful for views but is strenuous exercise and best suited to people in good physical condition. It ascends 3267 feet in 3.25 miles. If you choose to climb, certainly arm yourself with water, sunscreen, a hat and light rain jacket. Depart in the morning when thunderstorms are less prevalent. If you wish, stop at the gondola terminal for an optional sign-in, then ascend the trail just left of the terminal and follow the green disks marking the route to the top. The trail passes in and out of trees, up ski slopes and over dirt roads. Drinking water is available from an outdoor tap at about the halfway point. Picnic tables and a side trip to a scenic rocky bluff are just short of the summit. As the steep descent can be hard on knees and ankles, take advantage of the free gondola ride back to town. If you decide to hike down after riding up, walk toward Aspen from the restaurant and look for a sign for Silver Bell. Follow the arrow downhill to the right.

The mountain is known locally as "Ajax" for an old mine on its slope. If you hike, stay clear of any shafts or debris you discover. In the silver boom years, over 2000 miners and business folk functioned a few hundred feet below the mountain's summit in a thriving village called Tourtelotte Park. The community once bragged of more voters and more saloons than Aspen, but this swagger was probably overstatement.

The Silver Queen Gondola is not without **ancestors**. In the 1880s ore was hauled downhill by mule and bucket tramway from Hank Tourtelotte's Buckhorn claim on Aspen Mountain. For a price, local citizens could ride the ore buckets up and down the mountain. Sixty years later, Aspen's first vacationing skiers were hauled uphill by the "boat tow," a sled contraption, jerry-built from old mining equipment and a Model A Ford engine.

Mining is not just history in Aspen. The Compromise Silver Mine operates today at the top of the Little Nell ski run. Tours are available for both the Compromise and for the Smuggler Mine on the mountain across town.

A four-wheel-drive road to Aspen Mountain's peak is open to private vehicles in summer. Access is at the top of Original Street. The uphill journey covers 4.6 miles.

Rio Grande Trail
The Options

THE MULTIFACETED RIO GRANDE TRAIL IS AN EXCELLENT STARTING POINT FOR visitors to the Aspen area. It makes a fine first-day excursion because of its moderate elevation, its flat terrain, its proximity to town and its many access and exit points. It is appropriate for all ages and fitness levels. Choose from a short, paved eastern leg; a longer, paved central section; a woodsy nature loop option to the mid-trail; and an unpaved lower route through a canyon. The boisterous Roaring Fork River unifies it all with its voice, its bends, its bridges. Fishing is good. Bicyclists are permitted on all but the nature loop, and runners use this as a workout trail.

An overview map of all local Aspen trails stands at each of the Rio Grande's major access points: Herron Park, Puppy Smith Street and Cemetery Lane/Slaughterhouse Bridge. Note that walkers on the nature path may enter or exit at the Bayer-Benedict Music Tent or Aspen Meadows, thereby adding a stroll through Aspen's historic and charming West End. For a one-way hike on the upper portion, ride the free Cemetery Lane bus from Rubey Park to its final stop near Slaughterhouse Bridge and then walk back to central Aspen on the trail. Consult individual hike descriptions for details.

Upper Rio Grande Loop Hike

GENERAL AREA:	Aspen
TRAILHEAD:	2 blocks from Mill & Main in Aspen
	8.9 miles from rodeo in Snowmass Village
HIKING DISTANCE:	3.5 miles round trip from Puppy Smith St.
	4.0 miles round trip from Herron Park
ELEVATION LOSS:	140-180 feet
LOW POINT:	7700 feet at Slaughterhouse Bridge
HIGH POINT:	7840 feet at Puppy Smith Street trailhead
	7880 feet at Herron Park trailhead
HIGHLIGHTS:	The Roaring Fork, a constant presence
	A plethora of bridges spanning the river
	An optional, quiet nature loop
	A variety of access points
	An extension on the lower Rio Grande Trail
FISHING:	Mountain whitefish in river
	Rainbow, brown and brook trout in river
NEARBY ATTRACTIONS:	Aspen!

Comments: The upper Rio Grande Trail offers something for everyone. It begins at a park and children's playground; its paved, level route is popular with locals and visitors for walking, running and biking; and its quiet, unpaved up-and-down nature loop is reserved for pedestrians only. The entire trail parallels the Roaring Fork River and generally follows the old narrow-gauge Denver & Rio Grande Railroad bed. Water music is a constant pleasure. The woodsy nature section lies across the river, connected to the main route by two bridges, and has sidetrails to the Bayer-Benedict Music Tent and to Aspen Meadows. Some homes hug the riverbank or sit above the trail. Respect this nearby private property by keeping to the path. The sun can be hot at midday; a hat and water bottle are recommended. Choose from access points on the east side, in downtown Aspen and behind the Music Tent in the West End.

Aspen to Trailhead(s): For the complete river walk, begin at Herron Park in southeast Aspen by taking Main Street four blocks east to Neal Street, which angles left just where Main makes a sharp right turn to become Original Street. Drop downhill over "No Problem Bridge" to the park and trailhead.

For access from midtown, walk downhill on Mill Street from Main, passing alongside the Hotel Jerome. At the second street, Puppy Smith, turn left and look for a Rio Grande Trail sign and a path to the right just opposite the post office. A large overview map and a second, newer trail entrance are 100 yards farther along Puppy Smith. From here you can walk downriver 1.75 miles to Slaughterhouse Bridge or you can walk upriver a quarter-mile to Herron Park.

Trail Route: The short section of trail from Herron Park to the post office begins with a large map defining the main route downriver and noting many deadend spurs. The park has picnic tables, interesting play equipment for children and river shallows for wading. Begin on a paved path and cross the lively Roaring Fork on a long wooden bridge. Continue past a right turnoff leading to homes on the opposite bank. Walk through little Newbury Park, graced by benches, and alongside small ponds. Just beyond the sculpture of the Art Park, bear right downhill. Tred the Ron Krajian Bridge over the river to the red brick Aspen Art Museum, a building which originally served as a hydroelectric power plant. Walk by a stagnant pond, under the stone Mill Street bridge and over an arched metal bridge, again spanning the Roaring Fork. This is an artistic, sinuous path, well-designed to complement the beautiful river.

A trail junction near a large settling pond and rail fence marks the midtown access point from the post office on Puppy Smith Street. The pond and an ancient boiler resting in the grass mark the site of a 19th century lumber mill run by a plucky widow named Jenny Adair. Signs state your location, directing you downriver to continue your hike. Cross two wooden bridges in quick succession. Houses are visible across the river to your left, screened somewhat by tall willows, spruces and pines. Signs designating the distance traveled are posted along the route, and handsome wooden benches are placed at regular intervals. This is a most civilized trail.

Just beyond the half-mile marker are a bench and two hitching posts for bicycles. Here, too, is an arched footbridge spanning the river and signs on the left indicating the first access point to the pedestrian-only nature path, the Music Tent and the Meadows. Cross the river here or continue ahead to the second access point or to Slaughterhouse Bridge at Cemetery Lane, the terminus of the paved, upper Rio Grande.

About a half-mile ahead is another arched bridge, the second connecting point to the nature path. Signs say "The Meadows" and "8th Street." Cross here to loop back toward town on an undulating dirt footpath. Numerous brown and yellow signs along the way direct you to a variety of West End locations before the loop is completed at the first arched bridge, named Grindley Bridge.

At the crossing and at several points along the peaceful, shady nature path, short spurs take you to water's edge. In spots, simple plank benches are installed within feet of the river. The track is narrow, occasionally rocky, and winds between tall grasses and aspens. Primitive horsetail plant is in every damp place. Signs at a trail junction indicate that the right fork leads uphill to the Music Tent and Aspen Meadows. The climb is steep but very short. To return to downtown via the Rio Grande, bear left and soon step over the Grindley Bridge.

Should you wish to reach the end point of the paved Rio Grande before backtracking to the nature loop, continue to Cemetery Lane, a little more than a half-mile beyond the second turnoff for the nature path. Bright red walls and overhanging cliffs appear ahead, the colorful and dramatic scenery of the unpaved lower Rio Grande Trail. Another overview trail map stands at the Cemetery Lane access point, and a privy is across the road in a parking area serving hikers and fishermen using the downriver extension.

If you have energy and sufficient drinking water, explore the beautiful area beyond this point. The first mile is especially memorable.

Wilderness: none   USGS map: Aspen

Lower Rio Grande Hike

GENERAL AREA:	Aspen
TRAILHEAD:	2.1 miles from Mill & Main in Aspen
	8.8 miles from rodeo in Snowmass Village
HIKING DISTANCE:	2.0 miles round trip
ELEVATION LOSS:	100 feet
LOW POINT:	7600 feet at canyon's end
HIGH POINT:	7700 feet at Slaughterhouse Bridge trailhead
HIGHLIGHTS:	Dramatic river canyon scenery
	A feeling of remoteness near town
	Abundant fishing spots along a feisty river
	Optional hike extension to Woody Creek
FISHING:	Mountain whitefish in river
	Rainbow, brown and brook trout in river
NEARBY ATTRACTIONS:	Aspen!

Comments: The unpaved lower Rio Grande Trail is a continuation of the paved path that begins in town. It parallels the Roaring Fork River from Slaughterhouse Bridge in Aspen to McLain Flats Road in Woody Creek, a distance of 3.75 miles. The level, dirt trail follows the old narrow-gauge Denver & Rio Grande Railroad bed. The highly recommended first mile is through a canyon and is wonderfully scenic. Later, the trail opens up to sunlight and sagebrush as it meanders toward Woody Creek. Keep close to small children as the river is wild in places; bring water, as always, and wear any comfortable shoes. Picnic and fishing spots abound. Runners, walkers and bicyclists share this trail.

Aspen to Trailhead: Access the trail by foot from the upper Rio Grande, by the Cemetery Lane bus from central Aspen to Red Butte Drive or by car. If driving, go west on Main Street (Route 82) one mile from Mill and Main to Cemetery Lane. Turn right at the traffic light across from a golf course and drive an additional 1.1 miles downhill to Slaughterhouse Bridge and a parking area on the left.

Trail Route: The paved upper Rio Grande Trail passes under the bridge and turns to dirt at Henry Stein Park where the lower route begins. Fishermen often gather here where the Roaring Fork is broad and lively with its Class Four rapids. Walk through the park past a bench, a picnic table and a small, muddy pond. Another bench and table are tucked in trees a few steps farther along. The path is wide and flat with ample room for both bicyclists and walkers.

This gentle trail can seem far from civilization. The only sound is that of the tumultuous river. Yellow sweet clover perfumes the air in midsummer, replacing spring's wild roses. Tiny sidestreams trickle down cliffs. The sunny path leads to towering red bluffs which tilt toward the water, overhanging the route. Spruces and cottonwoods edge the trail, with the largest trees nearest the water. There are scrub oaks, tall grasses, many shrubs. But the best feature is the Roaring Fork, thundering around boulders and splattering over small rocks. Couples find this place romantic, but parents should guide young children away from some drop-offs above the water.

Across the river, the rock bluffs of Red Butte are strongly vertical. Tall and stately groves of slender conifers alternate with bare cliffs, which are first red, then gray. The scenery is altogether splendid.

Less than a mile from the hike's start sits a stagnant pond cluttered with fallen timber. Here the trail narrows, and the land drops softly to riverbank, allowing easy descent to water's edge. The canyon is behind you as the cliffs on the left are replaced by hillsides carpeted with low vegetation. Sagebrush grows in this bright place, adding its scent to that of the sweet clover.

A bridge spans the river, and buildings of a power plant rest on a hillside beyond. The bridge is accessed after first passing above it on the trail. If you cross and turn right, the trail leads to the rear of the Aspen Airport Business Center, where bus service is available; if you cross and turn left, the trail ends where Maroon Creek tumbles into the Roaring Fork.

Hike Extension: If you continue on the Rio Grande Trail beyond the Business Center, be certain to carry adequate water as this open territory is hot and dry. At 3.75 miles from your start at Slaughterhouse Bridge, you reach McLain Flats Road, the Upper Woody Creek Bridge and Jaffee Park in Woody Creek. Smith Way and Upper River Road also intersect here.

Elevation here is 7400 feet, a loss of 300 feet from the trailhead. Near the trail's end is a parking place for fishermen just steps from the Roaring Fork. The cold river and adjacent spruces and cottonwoods provide welcome natural air conditioning. Many cyclists ride the Rio Grande Trail to reach the Woody Creek Tavern, a colorful local gathering place on Upper River Road about a mile west of the trail's end.

Wilderness: none   USGS map: Aspen

Play Ball!

Old Aspen was addicted to baseball. Americans wild for the game brought it to the remote mountain wilderness 20 years after its invention. Quickly baseball became Aspen's favorite sport, holding a preeminent place in the mining camp's social life. A team was organized in the summer of 1881 and generated ardent support in weekend competitions against nines from the Independence and Ashcroft camps. Amateur leagues emerged, merchants stocked all manner of baseball equipment, and, by the second summer, town businesses were sponsoring teams such as the "Duffers" and the "Frontiers" for the Aspen Baseball Club. By then, baseball fanatics also had their detractors who complained of inebriation and profanity at games.

But for Aspen's working men and women, baseball remained the central summer diversion. By 1888 the town boasted a semiprofessional team which traveled to Denver, Pueblo, Leadville and Grand Junction. Fifteen-hundred zealous fans were customary at games, and Aspen newspapers reported contests in detail, upstaging mining news during the short season. Everything about each player's health, record and style received scrutiny. A victory over the big city Denver team was especially relished. After all, civic pride was at stake.

Amateur softball leagues flourish in the valley today, attracting business sponsors, celebratory enthusiasts and faithful media coverage. The semipros may have vanished, but participatory passion lives on.

Shadow-Aspen Mountain Loop Hike

GENERAL AREA:	Aspen
HOPKINS TRAILHEAD:	Eight blocks from Mill & Main in Aspen
	8.2 miles from rodeo in Snowmass Village
HIKING DISTANCE:	1.8 miles for basic loop
ELEVATION GAIN:	480 feet
LOW POINT:	7920 feet at trailhead
HIGH POINT:	8400 feet
HIGHLIGHTS:	Good view of Aspen
	Ripe serviceberries in August
	Easy hike extension
FISHING:	None
NEARBY ATTRACTIONS:	Aspen!

Comments: This little view trail has a level midsection and steep ascents at its access points. Adjacent to downtown Aspen, it links Shadow Mountain's woods to Aspen Mountain's open slopes. Some residents use it as a quick morning warm-up. The basic loop can be done as an aerobic workout in 30 minutes or less, as a steady walk in 40-45 minutes and as a stroll in 60 minutes. Though short and scenic, it is not for those who dislike sharp ups and downs. A simple extension across the base of Aspen Mountain lengthens the hike. (Some local maps designate this entire route as the "Aspen Mountain Trail." Note that the Loop is not the hike to the mountain's summit.)

Aspen to Trailhead: This trail is convenient for visitors without cars as they can begin at the top end of S. Aspen Street next to Lift 1A or a few blocks away at S. Fourth Street and W. Hopkins Avenue. For those who drive to town, the best parking is at the parking garage on Mill Street, at Fourth and Hopkins, a half-mile SW of Mill and Main, or near Koch Lumber Park at E. Cooper and S. Garmisch. (East Hopkins changes to West Hopkins at Garmisch Street.)

Trail Route: If you begin at Fourth and Hopkins just below Shadow Mountain, walk a few yards on what appears to be an old gravel road to the right of a large gray house. The wide path leads to nearby trees and to brown signs reading "Little Cloud Park," "No Camping" and "Closed to Motor Vehicles." These markers are visible from Hopkins. The nearby tailings are testimony to Aspen's mining past.

A footpath runs both left and right of these signs, just behind the residences that back up to the mountain. This neighborhood path is a shortcut into town and serves as part of the loop.

Move upward into the woods and quickly bear left at a metal gate in a flat area atop tailings. Focus on going uphill and ignore the many spurs all through this area. The steep dirt path is bordered by Douglas-firs and carpeted with cones and needles. Some logs placed to the trail's right retard erosion, and a steel cable just beyond them signals a switchback to the left.

Breaks in the firs allow fine views of Aspen as you climb. Red Mountain, speckled with large homes, is to the left across the valley; Smuggler Mountain, its famous silver mine and tailings sitting low on its flank, is to the right. A dirt road snakes up Smuggler. Between the two mountains is a green depression where the Hunter Creek trail ascends through trees to the gentle hanging valley above.

As conifers thin out, shrubs and gambel oaks predominate, and the path's grade moderates. In early summer, lupine, wild rose and yellow sweet clover bloom. In midsummer, look for bedstraw, aspen daisy, sulphurflower, penstemon and sego lily. In late summer, the many serviceberry bushes provide fruit. Walk between a few aspens to emerge into a grassy space with Aspen Mountain, distinct with its ski trails, directly ahead. Before you is a lift with a trail beneath it—the trail that continues the walk. The ski company's summer road is up to your right.

The trail intersects the road where a sign points right for "Norway" and left for "Summer Road" and "Silver Queen Gondola." Walk left, passing under the lift. About a hundred yards beyond the ski lift, where the gondola is visible, take a gravelly trail downhill to return to Aspen's streets. The grade is fairly steep and running shoes with good traction are recommended.

Lift 1A and Shadow Mountain condos sit at the bottom of the slope. Step onto the top end of S. Aspen Street and descend one block to Durant. Turn left and walk one block to the Koch Lumber Park with its sand volleyball courts; follow a footpath through the park and directly behind the Ice Garden and private homes to Fourth Street, the Little Cloud Park sign and the loop's end.

Alternate Trailhead: Begin at Lift 1A at the top of S. Aspen Street and complete the Shadow/Aspen Mountain Loop in reverse. After the initial uphill, bear right onto the ski company's road and keep a sharp lookout for a narrow dirt path through tall grasses and wildflowers. It is just short of both the trees and the "Norway" sign, and it is easy to miss.

Hike Extension and Alternate Trailhead #2: If you begin from Fourth and Hopkins and want an extension to your hike, do not drop down to S. Aspen Street but continue ahead on the ski road toward the Silver Queen Gondola. When you are directly beneath the gondola, look for a well-worn path down to the Little Nell Hotel and Durant Street. The extension along the ski road with the return to Fourth Street adds 1.5 miles to the hike. The gondola is an alternate trailhead for the loop and is also the trailhead for the popular climb to the summit of Aspen Mountain.

Wilderness: none   USGS map: Aspen

Hunter Valley Loop Hike

General Area:	Aspen
Trailhead:	1.7 miles from Mill & Main in Aspen
	10.4 miles from rodeo in Snowmass Village
Hiking Distance:	4.2 miles round trip for Hunter Valley loop
Elevation Gain:	450 feet
Low Point:	8350 feet at Red Mountain parking area
High Point:	8800 feet in meadows
Highlights:	Views of Aspen and nearby mountains
	Pastoral mountain meadows with creek
	Ghost buildings and miners' cabins
	Easy hike extension
Fishing:	Colorado River cutthroat trout in creek
Nearby Attractions:	Aspen!

Comments: This access trail to Hunter Valley is an alternative to the Hunter Creek Trail. It requires 500 feet less elevation gain and is less rocky underfoot. It may be ideal for families introducing children to mountain hiking or for people desiring a less strenuous outing. The gentle loop at the top offers some fresh terrain, and more ambitious hikers can wander farther into Hunter Valley on either the north or south side of Hunter Creek. This open mountain valley permits exploration without danger of disorientation. Beaver ponds, picnic spots and ghost cabins abound, and early summer offers splendid wildflowers to enjoy.

Aspen to Trailhead: Drive north on Mill Street as it drops downhill to a bridge over the Roaring Fork River. Bear left on Red Mountain Road near the Aspen Art Museum. At 1.3 miles from Mill and Main, via winding Red Mountain Road, is Hunter Creek Road on the right. Turn right, dip slightly, and at 1.6 miles look for a blue sign saying "Hunter Creek Trailhead Parking Lot." After a sharp left into a horseshoe turn, look for another identical blue sign directing you right onto a gravel drive and into a parking area. A separate notice forbids overnight parking here. This lot is 1.7 miles from Mill and Main.

Trail Route: From the parking area backtrack on foot to a brown building, a structure belonging to the City of Aspen water treatment plant. Near it is posted a brown sign with white lettering reading "Hunter Creek Trail. Steep access." A contemporary gray house stands across from the trailhead.

Move left and uphill on the red dirt trail that winds through oaks, mountain mahogany, sagebrush and serviceberries. Below is the parking area. Downvalley rises Mount Sopris, and behind you are nice views of Aspen Mountain and the town itself. Many beautiful homes are perched nearby. The trail moderates then descends to two single spans of wooden fence marked with a blue diamond. Bear right to another length of fence, a gravel road, a paved road and two Hunter Creek trail signs. Walk the paved road toward two spans of fence, a brown trail sign and a blue diamond.

Take the soft dirt path downhill through low trees and shrubs. The increasing voice of Hunter Creek confirms that you are moving in the right direction. Almost immediately you are at Benedict Bridge and have merged with the Hunter Creek Trail—a trail which ascends through woods along the creek, crossing four bridges and many wooden walkways over marsh before it reaches this junction. The bridge is named for Aspen's celebrated Fritz Benedict, outdoorsman, architect and model citizen.

This creek crossing is particularly beautiful as a sidestream drops from high above and the water divides around an island, uniting as it flows under the bridge. Walk uphill on an old dirt road to the right of Hunter Creek. Keep alert. You must share this section of trail with mountain bikers. Douglas-firs, blue spruces and aspens line the road. Colorful Red Mountain is across the creek to the left. Smuggler Mountain is at your right.

Where the trail moderates and moves slightly away from water, you approach a junction. Choose the center route which winds through light woods on a narrow dirt path. (The left fork leads to private land over a private bridge, and the right fork heads toward Smuggler Mountain over more private property. Respect owners' rights.) A sign ahead states "Hunter Valley Trail No. 1992." A map again notes your proximity to trails that connect this valley to Red and Smuggler Mountains. This is an opportunity to choose your direction and distance if you seek adventure beyond the route described here.

Move ahead through a meadowy area on a flat sandy path toward what once was a municipal reservoir for the city of Aspen. A private home can be seen to the left. Aspens and lodgepole pines grow here and there, and lilac daisies blossom amidst grasses in mid to late summer. In earlier times ranchers grazed cows and sheep in this valley.

To the left is the Tenth Mountain Bridge over Hunter Creek. But continue straight ahead on a narrow path to the right of the water. You will make a loop, returning later across the Tenth Mountain Bridge. Far ahead, the peaks of the Williams Mountains appear to barricade the valley. The loop path here is flat and lends itself to travel with children or to a rapid pace for those seeking exercise. It is a fine running trail.

Move along through this spacious, pastoral place until reaching the old, primitive reservoir bridge spanning the creek at left. Ahead are some beaver dams and a small, attractive log cabin with a corrugated metal roof. You may wish to investigate. This is an especially pretty place for a pause, and the scenery and sound of water add to its charm. Farther down Hunter Valley at left stand the remains of another cabin. A old jeep track at right leads to Smuggler Mountain Road, which descends to Aspen. You have hiked about 1.75 miles from the trail intersection just before Benedict Bridge.

Step across the rustic span, bear left, and begin a lovely walk through a huge meadow. In this grassy place grow an astonishing number of corn lilies/false hellebores. Their size makes them hard to miss. They signal damp conditions. White field daisies and harebells combine for a midsummer show. Willows edge the creek. The walking is easy.

This meadow is also home to a collection of old ranch buildings. Several dwellings and a shed still stand while the largest structure, at the meadow's far end, has tumbled down. Black and white signs on the buildings say "Keep Out. Private Property." The structures are in weakened condition and, though picturesque, should be avoided. The view ahead includes the ski mountains and, beyond them, the peaks of the Maroon Bells-Snowmass Wilderness. A sign indicates you are still on Hunter Valley Trail No. 1992. To complete the valley loop and return to the Tenth Mountain Bridge, avoid the sidetrails to the right.

Continue across meadowland until spotting a sign for the bridge on the left; cross it and connect with the trail you hiked earlier. Bear right to return to your start. On your return trip, turn right just beyond Benedict Bridge. Follow the path, cross a road and walk over rolling terrain to the parking area on Red Mountain.

Hike Extension: The sylvan, quiet beauty of Hunter Valley rewards those who continue east toward the Williams Mountains. At the far end of the loop you have two choices: Instead of crossing the reservoir bridge, walk forward for about a mile or until the trail fades; or traverse the bridge and then turn right where a clear trail parallels the water for about two miles. The many beaver constructions are impressive, and the meadows, wildflowers, butterflies and birds make the extension a pleasure.

Wilderness: none   USGS map: Aspen

Hunter Valley

Pretty, pastoral Hunter Valley has always been a rather quiet retreat from Aspen. Miners did some exploration, but as the land was outside the main vein of silver ore, little came of their efforts. Instead, the gentle meadows were settled by ranchers who raised cattle and milk cows, helping to sustain town residents well into the 20th century. Buildings from an original homestead, the Bullock ranch, cluster today alongside the hiking trail and creek. Two lumber mills operated in the valley, providing timber for mines and homes, and tumbling Hunter Creek powered a hydroelectric plant. The plant's handsome brick structure now houses the Aspen Art Museum, and a crude bridge in the valley marks remnants of an old reservoir. A school served the settlers' children.

In the 1930s the ranchers sold out to a Basque named Lamicq and his partner. The new owners raised sheep in Utah and brought them, first by the Denver & Rio Grande railroad and later by truck, to Hunter Valley for summer grazing. Basque herders were imported to tend the sheep. Domestic animals are gone now, and, through the efforts of farsighted citizens, much of the valley is reserved for outdoor recreation and wildlife. But a preservation movement will remain vibrant until all controversies over private land are resolved.

Hunter Creek Loop Hike

GENERAL AREA: Aspen
TRAILHEAD: 0.4 miles from Mill & Main in Aspen
9.1 miles from rodeo in Snowmass Village
HIKING DISTANCE: 5.5 miles round trip for Hunter Creek loop
ELEVATION GAIN: 950 feet
LOW POINT: 7850 feet at trailhead
HIGH POINT: 8800 feet in meadow
HIGHLIGHTS: Five bridges and tumbling water in woods
Pastoral mountain meadows with creek
Ghost buildings and miners' cabins
Views of the Elk and Williams Mountains
Serviceberries and thimbleberries in August
Easy hike extension
FISHING: Colorado River cutthroat trout in creek
NEARBY ATTRACTIONS: Aspen!

Comments: Though the approach to Hunter Valley via Hunter Creek is the more challenging route, it offers easy trailhead access by foot or bus and rewards travelers with a beautiful climb alongside a creek splashing through boulders. The gentle loop through meadows at the top offers variety, and ambitious hikers can wander farther into Hunter Valley on the north or south side of Hunter Creek. This open mountain valley allows exploration without danger of disorientation. Ghost cabins, picnic spots and beaver ponds abound, and early summer is a splendid time to enjoy wildflowers.

Aspen to Trailhead: Walk or bike north on Mill Street as it dips downhill to a bridge over the Roaring Fork River. Bear left on Red Mountain Road just over the bridge near the Aspen Art Museum. Take the first right onto Lone Pine Road and look for a brown sign saying "Hunter Creek Trail." The sign directs you toward some condominiums. If traveling by the free Hunter Creek bus, ask the driver to stop in front of the Hunter Creek condominiums.

Trail Route: Walk alongside a wooden fence edging a gravel path. Another sign specifies the activities permitted on this route: biking, horseback riding, skiing and walking. Dogs must be leashed, and motorized vehicles are prohibited. A map details the many trails that intersect in Hunter Valley.

Follow the path as it passes between condominium buildings and brings you immediately within sound and sight of Hunter Creek, bubbling and dashing around stones. Descend a few steps to a trail sign on the right. The fence ends here. Walk parallel to the water and tread a low wooden walkway across a sidestream joining Hunter Creek from the east. This is the first of many simple wood sidewalks that carry hikers over marshy areas.

The smooth dirt path winds through aspens and young spruces. Horsetail plant grows in this wet place, and white, round boulders are scattered everywhere. The creek tumbles down noisily at left. Some homes can be spied through the trees. A fence in front of you and to your right precedes the first of the five wooden bridges that make this trail distinctive and scenic.

Move left across the tidy bridge. All the trail's bridges are constructed with handrails. Hunter Creek rushes underneath, plummeting between rotund rocks toward the Roaring Fork River below.

Serviceberry bushes are abundant here, and in August they supply the gatherer with ripe fruit for pies, muffins, pancakes and conserves. In springtime, wild roses perfume this trail. Paintbrush and coneflowers follow. Thimbleberry bushes bear white flowers above their big broad leaves in early summer and offer raspberry-like fruits in late August.

The second bridge crosses a quiet sidestream making its way to Hunter Creek. The path opens up to sunshine and the sight of houses perched above. The creek babbles below to your right. The third bridge, angled midway, carries you over the main creek in a gorgeous spot where water crashes down on both sides of a large rockslide, creating double waterfalls.

After this third bridge the trail mounts uphill to the left. A sidetrail at right leads to the creekbank. Steps help with the climb. Continue uphill over some rocks and sandy soil. Walk through aspens and evergreens. There are many nice spots for water views. The entrance to bridge four is marked by obstructive rocks. The bridge is long and straight, and the creek is lovely, ornamented with boulders wearing orange-red lichen. The trail continues uphill over rough ground.

Walk among white firs and Douglas-firs. At a lookout point on the right are the remains of a wooden bridge and an installation that controls water flow. Ignore the several side trails at left. Soon the main trail is interrupted by massive rocks which you must climb on and around to reach bridge five, named Benedict Bridge for Aspen's celebrated Fritz Benedict, outdoorsman, architect and model citizen. Just beyond the rocky section and just before bridge five is a trail descending from the left. This is the access trail from Red Mountain to Hunter Valley. At this junction the Hunter Valley and Hunter Creek trails become one. You have hiked approximately one mile.

To continue, consult the trail description for the Hunter Valley Loop Hike. On your return trip, traverse the Benedict Bridge and continue downhill over the remaining four bridges to reach Lone Pine Road. Aspen comes into view after the second crossing.

Hike Extension: The sylvan, quiet beauty of Hunter Valley rewards those who continue east toward the Williams Mountains. At the far end of the loop you have two choices: Instead of crossing the reservoir bridge, walk forward for about a mile or until the trail fades; or traverse the bridge and then turn right where a clear trail parallels the water for about two miles. The many beaver constructions are impressive, and the gentle meadows, wildflowers, butterflies and birds make the extension a pleasure.

Wilderness: none   USGS map: Aspen

Sunnyside Hike

GENERAL AREA:	Aspen
TRAILHEAD:	2.5 miles from Mill & Main in Aspen
	9.2 miles from rodeo in Snowmass Village
HIKING DISTANCE:	3.7 miles round trip to antennas in woods
ELEVATION GAIN:	1600 feet to antenna towers
LOW POINT:	7800 feet at trailhead
HIGH POINT:	9400 feet at antenna towers in woods
HIGHLIGHTS:	View of Aspen, ski areas, RF Valley, peaks
	Aromatic scent of sagebrush
	Ripe serviceberries in August
FISHING:	None
NEARBY ATTRACTIONS:	Aspen!

Comments: This Red Mountain view trail carries hikers higher and higher above the Roaring Fork Valley via multiple switchbacks. It approaches private homes and crosses irrigation ditches as it twists uphill through sagebrush and scrub oaks. The trail is carefully marked, and the vista improves with each turn. As the path is not rocky, any basic athletic shoe is suitable. The truly fit person may run the trail for a superb workout. But it can be hot here. Hikers need water, a hat and sunscreen. Morning and evening excursions are recommended. In April and May when ticks are active in the brushy terrain, hikers should wear long sleeves, long pants and insect repellent.

Aspen to Trailhead: Sunnyside Trail is accessed by car, bus or bicycle. If driving, head west on Main Street in Aspen. Just beyond Castle Creek Bridge, turn right onto Cemetery Lane at a traffic light. A golf course lies across the intersection. Drive 1.5 miles, passing Red Butte Cemetery and crossing Slaughterhouse Bridge over the Roaring Fork River. The street's name changes to McLain Flats Road before reaching a parking area left of the road opposite Red Butte, an Aspen landmark. The distant view is of Mount Daly rising beyond Snowmass Village. The trailhead right of the road is designated by a large wooden placard, an arrow and spans of fencing.

The free Cemetery Lane bus from Aspen makes its final stop where Red Butte Drive meets Cemetery Lane, about a half-mile short of the trailhead. Walk uphill to the north. For cyclists, the level paved section of the Rio Grande Trail, accessed near the bottom of Mill Street, intersects with Cemetery Lane at Slaughterhouse Bridge. This route adds about two miles each way.

Trail Route: A small marker on a post at the trailhead reads "Sunnyside Trail No. 1987." A National Forest sign with a map is a few steps up.

The trail is distinguished by the pleasant, pungent smell of sagebrush. There are two varieties here: big sagebrush (*Artemisia tridentata*), a woody shrub with three-toothed, wedge-shaped leaves; and the smaller wild sagebrush (*Artemisia cana*), a variety with fine, soft, grasslike leaves. Both are colored a silvery gray-green. Nearby is orange Wyoming paintbrush, the fiery, parasitic companion of sage.

This mountainside wears other foliage characteristic of the semiarid environment:
gnarled Gambel oak, juniper, mountain mahogany and serviceberry.
Lupine blooms in purple
masses in early summer.
Scarlet fairy trumpet follows. August is a gilded
time with the flowering of
mountain goldenrod and rabbitbrush.

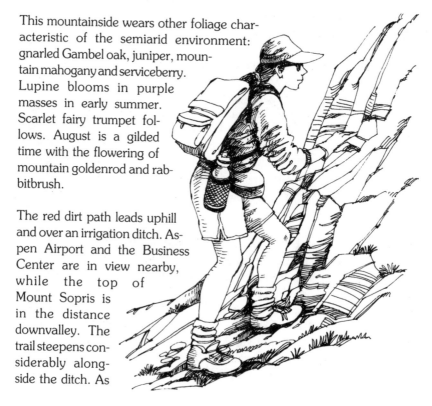

The red dirt path leads uphill
and over an irrigation ditch. Aspen Airport and the Business
Center are in view nearby,
while   the   top   of
Mount Sopris is
in the distance
downvalley. The
trail steepens con-
siderably along-
side the ditch. As

the path bends left, you see the ski runs of Aspen Mountain, the Highlands and Tiehack. With more climbing, peaks of the wilderness area gradually emerge from behind the ski slopes.

The trail edges the side of Red Mountain as it overlooks the Roaring Fork Valley. Three switchbacks, a cairn and two trail signs precede a second irrigation ditch. Ignore a path paralleling the water. Cross over the ditch on a board to continue the hike.

Ascend to the right toward Aspen. Left is a barbed wire fence, and ahead is a green metal gate which may be closed or wired open. From here you view a pond and the trail's parking area below. Walk straight toward a private home. Look for massive Pyramid Peak and for the top of Capitol Peak just left of Mount Daly. As you approach the house, the trail switchbacks twice more. Step up to a private driveway and cross it, moving slightly right to continue the trail. Guideposts here read "Sunnyside Trail No 1987."

Pass above the house where you can peer down Owl Creek Valley to Snowmass Village. Go through a second green metal gate. The trail meanders here, winding and rolling, and then turns left toward more homes, the airport and distant Mount Sopris.

As the trail becomes quite steep and the oaks diminish in size, providing no shade, three sharp turns bring you in sight of antennas on the crest of a hill. A rigorous climb carries you into an aspen grove where there is soft dirt and easy walking. The light shade is welcome on a sunny day. Under the trees at midsummer bloom many lilac aspen daisies, some white sego lilies and fragrant bedstraw. Turn around here or at a communication building near the antennas five minutes farther into the woods.

Long-distance hikers continue through aspens, climb another 500 feet, walk east to join the Hunter Valley Trail and descend into Aspen via Hunter Creek for a trip of about 10 miles. Many sidetrails may make this longer trip confusing. A good map is necessary.

Wilderness: none   USGS map: Aspen

# Ute Trail Hike

General Area: Aspen
Trailhead: 0.9 miles from Mill & Main in Aspen
9.6 miles from rodeo in Snowmass Village
Hiking Distance: 2.4 miles round trip
Elevation Gain: 1700 feet
Low Point: 8000 feet at trailhead
High Point: 9700 feet at rocky viewpoint
Highlights: Aerial look at Aspen
Great workout for energetic visitors
A vertical hike extension
Fishing: None
Nearby Attractions: Aspen!

Comments: Here is something for the truly fit person who craves an aerobic workout with a scenic reward. Heart, lungs and legs are asked to perform on this tough uphill. The steepness can be hard on knees on the return trip. The turnaround point is a rocky outcropping overlooking Aspen. Take water, as always, and consider this trail for a cool morning or evening until acclimated. Many active local residents exercise here and ascend in about 45 minutes.

Aspen to Trailhead: The location of this trailhead on Ute Avenue in southeast Aspen makes it available to visitors lacking transportation. If starting from Mill and Main, walk, bike or drive east on Main. As the street makes a major turn to the right, the name changes to Original and the street heads south toward Aspen Mountain. Where Original appears to end, make a sharp left onto Ute Avenue, located at the mountain's base. Continue ahead to the brown "Ute Trail" sign on the right just past Ajax Park and a green house. A parking area is opposite the trailhead. Additional spaces adjoin Ajax Park.

Ute Park, just below the trailhead, is dedicated to Aspen's original inhabitants, the Native Americans whose hunting trail has become today's

Ute Avenue. Adjacent to the park and partially hidden by tall grasses, Ute Cemetery holds gravestones of early Aspen settlers, including many Civil War veterans.

Trail Route: From the base of Aspen Mountain east of the ski slopes, look up to locate your destination: a rocky projection surrounded by evergreens. Resembling a ruined tower, the spot hovers directly above the trailhead. To its right, another crumbling turret protrudes from the forest. The stone-studded path begins at a brown sign and two single spans of wooden fencing.

Elevation is gained quickly as the Ute Trail ascends above the town via multiple short switchbacks. This is the antithesis of the flat Rio Grande Trail. Sun-loving aspens, oaks and berry bushes are soon replaced by tall evergreen spires as you climb. Snake up the mountain to the rocky outcropping—an aerial viewpoint guaranteed to give discomfort to hikers with acrophobia.

The scene below includes Aspen, the Roaring Fork River, Smuggler Mountain across the valley, and Red Mountain to Smuggler's left, or west. The trail to Hunter Valley twines up between these two broad peaks. Independence Pass is 20 miles east, and solitary Mount Sopris rises 30 miles to the west.

Hike Extension: If you want more of the same, head uphill and slightly west for about one-fourth mile to a ski trail and make your way to the summit of Aspen Mountain. The climb is merciless, but the panorama and restaurant at the top are definitely fine. And, best of all, hikers can hop on the Silver Queen Gondola for a free ride down the mountain. Additional elevation gain is 1512 feet. Aspen Mountain tops out at 11,212 feet.

Wilderness: none   USGS map: Aspen

Quaking Aspen
A Golden Voice

WHEN, IN 1880, PROMOTER B. CLARK WHEELER NAMED A RAW MINING camp "Aspen," he was inspired by the dense groves of slender trees that overspread the surrounding slopes. Mining and ski trails have reduced Aspen Mountain's leafy mantle, but these lithe, graceful poplars, widespread in North America, still impart visual beauty and sweet melody to this high valley.

An old story says that early French-Canadian trappers believed Christ's cross was made from aspen wood, causing the tree to tremble forevermore. An ancient belief in divination by means of leaves' sounds, called phyllomancy, must have given tremendous authority to the restless, rustling aspen. The precise message may be enigmatic, but most humans today take pleasure in the voice.

The most colorful tree in the Rockies, *Populus tremuloides* dresses for summer in bright green leaves that reveal their silvery undersides as they quiver and dance with every whiff of breeze. These roundish, gently toothed leaves flutter musically at the ends of long, flattened stalks. In autumn they flame brilliant yellow, gold, orange and, occasionally, scarlet. The tree's smooth, creamy white bark wears dark eye-shaped scars where limbs once grew. Sun is not only essential to the aspen's survival but is the ingredient that intensifies the tree's leaf colors, imparts gleam to its white bark, and creates the magical, dappled light beneath its branches. An aspen grove is a place of enchantment.

Native Americans of the mountains and woods needed only to rub their hands over the white trunks of aspen trees to obtain a **natural sunscreen**. Quaking Aspens wear a fine powdery coat to protect their thin soft bark from the intense ultraviolet light of high elevation. So what's an Aspen's SPF?

Intolerant of shade and losers in competition with conifers, trembling aspens clothe south-facing hillsides and wide meadows, leaving north slopes to the evergreens. Trees are 50 or

60 feet tall at maturity with trunks a foot thick. Individual aspens survive less than 100 years, though their extensive root system could be thousands of years old. Its buds, catkins, bark and fresh shoots sustain grouse, finches, porcupines, beavers, mule deer and elk. Gnawing, claws and knives damage aspen bark, resulting in permanent scarring and invasion by viruses that may eventually decimate an entire stand through the interconnected roots.

The Leafy Colossus

Forget blue whales, *Sequoia gigantea* and northern Michigan's 37 acre soil fungus. "The World's Largest Living Organism" is a stand of quaking aspens in Utah's Wasatch Mountains. In the West, aspens propagate asexually by root sprouts, cloning themselves by the thousands. Arising from the root of a single tree, a grove is technically one giant organism, with all trees greening up and gleaming gold together—often out-of-sync with the adjacent, unrelated stand. In 1993 the Utah grove had 47,000 stems, covered 106 acres and weighed perhaps 13.2 million pounds. Should the entire stand be cut or burned, its roots live on, sending up new sprouts again and again for untold generations.

The Roaring Fork River

BOTH THE ROARING FORK RIVER AND ITS FAMOUS TRIBUTARY, THE FRYINGPAN, carry the coveted Gold Medal Waters designation. The award recognizes waters with a superior aquatic habitat, with a large proportion of fish 14 inches or more in length, and with superb trophy trout fishing potential. Gold Medal Waters are restricted to artificial flies and lures, place limitations on the number and size of fish caught, and have catch-and-release sections. For details, consult with local outfitters or the Colorado Division of Wildlife.

The Roaring Fork courses 60 miles from its birth near the Continental Divide to the Colorado River at Glenwood Springs. Though quiet and accessible in places, it is also a rough and tumble canyon river with steep banks, swift currents, and moss-glazed rocks underfoot. It has big seasonal differences in temperature and flow rate. In the spring, gorged and unruly, the Roaring Fork woos river rafters. For an intimate look, walk the upper and lower Rio Grande Trail.

The river is stocked annually with 25,000 five-inch rainbow trout between Glenwood Springs and Aspen. Between Aspen and Independence Pass, 4800 ten-inch rainbows are added each year. Brown trout are abundant and stocked only when numbers fall. The ubiquitous brook trout is here, and the native mountain whitefish flourishes.

> Known to the Ute Indians as "Thunder River," the **Roaring Fork** was renamed by whites who apparently also recognized the river's headstrong, volatile nature.

MAROON BELLS

Wilderness
Maroon Bells Scenic Trail
Maroon-Crater Scenic Loop Hike
Pika
Indian Paintbrush
Fireweed

MAROON BELLS REGION

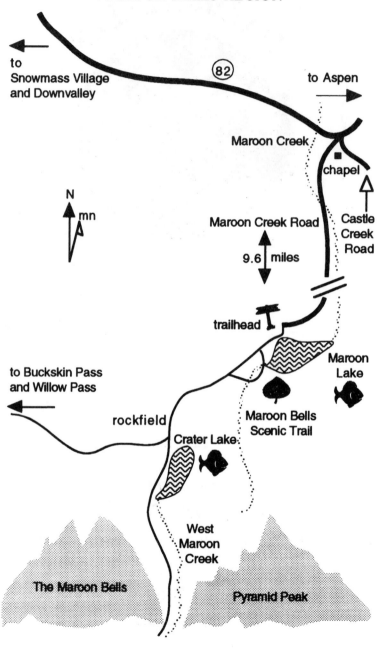

to
Snowmass Village
and Downvalley

to Aspen

82

Maroon Creek

chapel

N

mn

Maroon Creek Road

Castle
Creek
Road

9.6 miles

trailhead

Maroon
Lake

to Buckskin Pass
and Willow Pass

rockfield

Maroon Bells
Scenic Trail

Crater Lake

West
Maroon
Creek

The Maroon Bells

Pyramid Peak

Wilderness

WILDERNESS. THE WORD ELICITS IMPRESSIONS, NOSTALGIA AND FERVOR— even in people never exposed to untamed natural places. Do we humans possess an inherited memory for something familiar to our ancestors? Does our response reveal our genetic kinship to other life forms? Why does the idea of wilderness awaken longing in modern man? And why does it provoke emotional controversy?

Author Wallace Stegner voiced a belief in this connection to virgin sanctuaries when he wrote, "Something will have gone out of us as a people if we ever let the remaining wilderness be destroyed...." A century earlier, naturalist Henry David Thoreau expressed conviction: "In wildness is the preservation of the world." Do we, in protecting wildness, protect something irreplaceable inside ourselves?

Philosophers, perhaps, have always posed such questions. Through their concerned activism, environmentalists, educators and pragmatists have guaranteed that the debate may continue. Passage of the Wilderness Act of 1964 secured "... for the American people of present and future generations the benefits of an enduring resource...." Included in the Act is a definition by Howard Zahniser, once executive director of the Wilderness Society: "A wilderness is hereby recognized as an area where the earth and its community of life are untrammeled by man, where man himself is a visitor who does not remain."

Without roads, power lines, dams, logging, campgrounds and resorts, these refuges beckon to hikers, climbers, fishermen, equestrians, naturalists and photographers. Most find solitude and splendor. Primeval wilderness serves as an outdoor classroom and as a venue for both personal and scientific discovery. From Florida to Alaska, feral lands as varied as the continent are shielded from man's tampering.

But the Act's proponents found compromises to be necessary. Land preservation was, and continues to be, a controversial idea. Domestic cattle

Wilderness Care

Visitors to wilderness areas are asked to treat these special sanctuaries with the care reserved for their own most precious possessions. The guiding principle is to leave no trace of passage. Sign in at trailheads so that each region's use can be measured. Keep dogs leashed in consideration of wildlife and other visitors. Leave all mechanized equipment at home, including mountain bikes. Keep groups on trails to protect the fragile growth underfoot and to minimize erosion. Let your camera preserve memories of wildflowers, granting them continuance. Maintain the quiet presence of native birds and mammals. Know where and where not to camp or build fires. Carry out all that you carry in. And while human priorities are secondary here, human needs may be satisfied, for nature can rejuvenate the most world-weary soul.

and sheep, unnatural to the wilderness, graze within its boundaries. Some mining interests received consideration when the Act was crafted. Proposals for additional wild acreage consistently meet with opposition from those who view natural resources as marketable commodities. Nonetheless, the National Wilderness Preservation System has expanded tenfold since its original nine million acres were set aside in "an unimpaired condition."

Aspen is fortunate in its location. Cloistered in a remote mountain valley, it slumbered while other western towns metamorphosed into cities. Grand tracts of surrounding land, rugged and inaccessible, invited few intruders. As wilderness preservation caught the public's attention, Aspen emerged as a desirable launch point for outdoor experiences rich with beauty and challenge. Personal humility and a respect for nature have become inevitable by-products. The Maroon Bells-Snowmass Wilderness is a brilliant jewel in the wilderness crown. Neighboring gems are the Hunter-Fryingpan and Collegiate Peaks wild areas, and only slightly more removed are the Holy Cross, Raggeds and Mount Massive wilderness tracts.

To modern explorers, these primitive enclaves are more than a connection to the continent's history. They are places to find balance and perspective in today's world. But ecologist Aldo Leopold knew early in the 20th century that "... the richest values of wilderness lie not in the days of Daniel Boone, nor even in the present, but rather in the future."

Maroon Bells Scenic Trail

THE MAROON BELLS SCENIC TRAIL IS SITUATED IN ONE OF THE LOVELIEST PLACES in North America. The beauty is obvious as you wend gently downhill to Maroon Lake through an enormous wildflower meadow. At times you step over trickles of water, snowmelt from the massive mountains and ridges dominating the skyline. Follow the dirt trail along the right shore of the lake. Pass a classic beaver lodge and walk under quaking aspens to a sign placed by the U.S. Forest Service for the "Scenic Trail No. 2197 and Beaver Pond." Here is a pastoral path rich with flora, fauna, quiet ponds and the melody of a bustling creek.

This nature trail's options include either one or two bridges and both a long and short loop. Explore on your own or join a naturalist for a free guided walk. The Aspen Center for Environmental Studies, in cooperation with the Forest Service, conducts walks on the hour from 10 a.m. to 2 p.m. from mid-June through early September. ACES staffs a powerful telescope from 10 a.m. until 3 p.m. to help visitors discover bighorn sheep, elk, eagles and other cliff-dwellers. This trail is suitable for all family members. Elevation at Maroon Lake is 9580 feet.

Aspen to Destination: See directions to the Maroon-Crater Scenic Loop.

Silver prospectors were disappointed in their exploration of the **Maroon Creek Valley**, but ranchers and lumbermen settled in, satisfied with other natural resources—grass and trees. The pioneers of the 1880s raised cattle and some sheep. One of the two original large spreads in the valley, the Sievers homestead, is today's T-Lazy-7 Ranch. A few mills supplied lumber to Aspen and the mining companies. The gentle East Maroon Trail follows an old stagecoach route linking Aspen to Gothic. Built in 1884, the toll road was for sale by 1887 when two railroad construction projects promised to connect secluded Aspen more comfortably to the outside nation.

Maroon-Crater Scenic Loop Hike

GENERAL AREA: Maroon Creek Valley
TRAILHEAD: 10.9 miles from Mill & Main in Aspen
17.0 miles from rodeo in Snowmass Village
HIKING DISTANCE: 3.6 miles round trip for lake and loop
3.2 miles round trip to Crater Lake only
ELEVATION GAIN: 496 feet
LOW POINT: 9580 feet at Maroon Lake
HIGH POINT: 10,076 feet at Crater Lake
HIGHLIGHTS: Two lakes and a sparkling creek
Broad flowery meadows
Smashing views of three fourteeners
A beaver lodge, pikas, ground squirrels
A scenic, alternate return route
Optional hike extension
FISHING: Rainbow trout in Maroon Lake
Colorado River cutthroat trout in Crater Lake
Brook trout in West Maroon Creek
NEARBY ATTRACTIONS: Aspen!

Comments: The Maroon Lake-Crater Lake Scenic Loop has just about everything necessary for a rich introduction to the Colorado mountains: towering peaks worthy of countless rolls of film; meadows and hillsides with coverlets of wildflowers; a boulderfield alive with pikas, marmots and ground squirrels; aspen woods of dappled sunshine and the flutter of birds; a dashing, whitewater creek dropping in small waterfalls; ponds lying adjacent to a beaver lodge; trout gliding through cool waters. The direct trail between the lakes is extremely popular but bypasses the lovely alternate return route. Yet many visitors underestimate even the simpler excursion and set off without water, athletic shoes or protective clothing for sun or rain. These same visitors often depart in the afternoon when mountain weather can be fickle. For a leisurely, pleasurable trip, make adequate preparations and start your adventure in the morning.

Aspen to Trailhead: Drive west from Aspen on Route 82. At 1.3 miles from Mill and Main, make a left turn onto Maroon Creek Road at a chapel and traffic light. Stay right at the immediate fork and continue for 9.6 miles to Maroon Lake where signs direct you to a parking area. Privies and drinking water are nearby. To protect the valley's fragile ecosystem, Maroon Creek Road is closed to incoming private vehicular traffic between 8:30 a.m. and 5:00 p.m. Frequent bus transportation from Aspen's parking garage and Rubey Park terminal is available. Bicycles are always permitted on Maroon Creek Road.

Trail Route: Depart the parking area by one of many soft dirt footpaths that traverses the expansive meadow above Maroon Lake. Walk through tall grasses and flowers. At midsummer look for cow parsnip, delphinium, mertensia/chimingbells, fireweed, Richardson's geranium and orange sneeze-weed. Small rivulets of water slip across the paths as you meander through the meadow. The Maroon Bells, the adjacent fourteeners so linked to Aspen's identity, are directly in front of you, and Pyramid Peak, another mountain over 14,000 feet, is to the left. All three are dramatic in color and form.

Pass right of Maroon Lake and move through quaking aspens to signs placed by the U.S. Forest Service. For a short nature walk follow "Scenic Trail No. 2197 and Beaver Pond" to the left. To reach Crater Lake follow "Maroon-Snowmass Trail No. 1975" to the right. Delicate blue harebells and lavender aspen daisies bloom here, mingling with the meadow flowers. The dome of a perfect beaver lodge protrudes above the lake's teal surface. Step over a sidestream as you again enter aspens where you find more wooden signs. Here is a second cutoff for the scenic trail, which stays low near Maroon Lake, and another sign for Maroon-Snowmass Trail to Crater Lake and beyond. To the path's right is a Maroon-Snowmass Wilderness boundary marker. Beyond this marker and in all wilderness areas, dogs must be leashed. Dogs are banned completely from Crater Lake environs.

A footbridge is below the trail. It spans a creek and is part of the nature trail and scenic loop that is an option on the return trip. Beaver ponds are also visible as you walk. The main trail is rocky and uneven, requiring that you pick up your feet. The hillside at right blocks views, but the valley, creek and ponds can be glimpsed at left through trees. The climb becomes more challenging as it continues over a rough surface, carrying you through a small rockslide area high above the valley. Pyramid Peak, craggy and imposing, dominates the skyscape.

Once more a sign points left for the Scenic Trail and ahead for Maroon-Snowmass Trail. Another sign warns: "Travelers above this point should prepare for sudden changes in weather and difficult terrain." *On your return from Crater Lake, it is here that you should leave the main trail to enjoy the optional scenic loop back to Maroon Lake.*

The trail angles right as it mounts uphill. Blue spruces, white firs, Douglas-firs and common junipers mix with aspens. Bush honeysuckle berries, white dotted saxifrage and orange paintbrush grow in sunlit patches. The trail switchbacks into a capacious, rock-filled basin.

The rocky basin is a fascinating place to linger. Pointed spires top a picturesque jagged wall. Tall, dark conifers growing just below the crest mimic the spires. Look for a lovely, slender cascade dropping in front of the magnificent Maroon Bells. Snow persists in several high bowls, giving contrast and definition to the mountains. Photographers can be happy here.

Common flowers along this trail are woolly groundsels, with gray-green fuzzy leaves and clustered heads of small yellow flowers. Here among the rocks they are intermixed with blue columbines, golden shrubby cinquefoil, wild strawberries and raspberries. And sometimes an observant flower-lover can spy a rare red columbine. Nearby are the pale, frosted, berrylike cones of the prickly common juniper. Rub them to find strong color beneath the white powder. Lichen in a vivid chartreuse grows atop the stones.

Many pikas dwell here and an alert lookout will herald your arrival with a nasal "eehk." Golden-mantled ground squirrels are omnipresent, and a yellow-bellied marmot may survey you from a sun-warmed boulder. Pause, remain still and quiet, and these beguiling creatures will reveal much about themselves.

Sedimentary rocks in the basin are brightly multicolored; their stripes write their geologic biographies. There are red-orange layers in blue-green rocks. Black ribbons alternate with bands of red or white. All tell of prehistoric changes in the Earth. This is fodder for the amateur geologist.

Walk forward to a space devastated by a 1993 avalanche. Snow thundered across the trail from the steep ridge at right, bending and breaking trees, sweeping some away, and leaving others in jumbled piles. Here is dramatic evidence of the muscle of moving snow. Recovery will be slow in this land of brief summers.

The route is distinct as it dips and rises through the rockfield. The rough footing is mitigated by thick-soled athletic shoes or hiking boots. Ahead, you can see a large notch left of the twin Bells. This is West Maroon Creek Valley—U-shaped, sculpted by glaciers. Crater Lake is in sight as you come over the last small rise in the basin. Then the trail drops gently down through airy woods to signs at a junction. Follow "West Maroon Trail No. 970." An arrow points ahead toward Crater Lake. "Maroon-Snowmass Trail No. 1975" to the right leads sharply uphill to high-rise Buckskin and Willow Passes. A registry box is here for long-distance hikers, and rules are posted for campers and dog owners. No dogs are permitted at the lake; they must stay on the trail and move along quickly.

Walk to the water through a meadow dotted with spruces, firs and junipers. Fallen trees are jammed together at the near end of the lake. Conifers on shore create dark green reflections. The narrow cascade dropping from the Bells adds music while chimingbells, brookcress, sorrel and green gentian add art. Ground squirrels frolic underfoot with hope of handouts. Advance a bit for improved views of the waterfall and of West Maroon Creek valley, barricaded at its terminus by a giant snowy ridge. The trail twists ahead between shrubby willows and under cool conifers before it meanders up the valley to West Maroon Pass. Almost everywhere are scree slopes where rock has broken free and piled up below cliffs. These are precipitous, breakaway mountains.

On the return trip you may wish to extend the hike into a loop by treading over new territory. When you reach the junction where the creek, beaver ponds, log jam and Maroon Lake are visible below, check the signs, and take the "Scenic Trail" to the right. (This is the intersection where a notice warns of changeable weather and difficult terrain.)

The early section of this sidetrail is a plunge down a hillside—more challenging than the Maroon Lake trail. But quickly the grade moderates, and you approach a guidepost which points in two directions. If you continue forward, you will get to Maroon Lake by passing left of the beaver ponds and just below the Maroon-Snowmass Trail. For a highly recommended outdoor experience, turn right to take a slightly longer but much prettier way back to Maroon Lake. There is a bridge partway along the loop for an early crossing over the creek to the more direct route.

By picking the right fork you skirt the far side of the beaver ponds. This is a lush locale with tall undergrowth below the aspens. From the dirt path, you soon hear water and see it emerge from under rocks and willows. A creek has bubbled out—seeming to spring literally from the earth to begin a mad dash to Maroon Lake.

Nearby, you can view a pond's bottom through the clear water. A small, adjacent meadow is lit with fireweed and florescent orange paintbrush. Moisture and mountain sunshine encourage a bounty of wildflowers and berry bushes. As you pass among some aspens, the trail is narrow in places and nearly overgrown with rangy plants. It shepherds you to a special viewsite where the divided creek spawns four waterfalls. Move farther down the trail to a bridge which conveys you to a wonderful spot directly over this turbulent creek, blue-white in its haste to reach the lake. You can traverse this bridge to the direct route of the scenic trail or can continue on the right side of the creek across more flowery fields until encountering another bridge at the upper end of Maroon Lake. Fishermen often select this location.

Cross this second bridge over calm water to return to the hike's start. Choose from a variety of paths through the meadow to the parking area.

Hike Extensions: Crater Lake is the jumping-off place for longer hikes to Buckskin and Willow Passes via Maroon-Snowmass Trail No. 1975 and to West Maroon Pass via West Maroon Trail No. 1970. The West Maroon Trail, which edges Crater Lake before passing through a grove of trees, is quite gentle for its first mile as it winds between massive "fourteeners." Turn back at the crossing point for West Maroon Creek for a round trip of about five miles. *The Aspen Dayhiker* describes several challenging hikes in this area.

Wilderness: Maroon Bells-Snowmass   USGS map: Maroon Bells

Pika
Rockfield Ventriloquist

A PIKA IS SOMETHING OF A PHANTOM. WHILE HIS SHRILL METALLIC BLEAT IS a real attention-grabber, the nasal "eehk" seems misplaced, ventriloquial. And his mottled brown-gray fur and his rotund shape make him indistinguishable from the tumble of rocks he calls home. But when the little Pika moves, skittering effortlessly over boulders and talus slides, he provides fascinating entertainment and a good excuse to pause on the trail.

Looking much like a guinea pig, the engaging Pika is the smallest member of the Lagomorph order, making him a relative of rabbits and hares. But, unlike his cousins, *Ochotona princeps* has short rounded ears, no visible tail and stubby, non-jumping hindlegs. He lives in sociable colonies in the rockfields of western mountains, usually between 8500 and 13,500 feet. Fleeter, more nimble and more energetic than his indolent marmot neighbor, the Pika industriously gathers nearby wildflowers, grasses and sedges and spreads them out to cure in low "haystacks" partially sheltered by boulders. These piles of drying vegetation signal Pika territory, as do spots of sticky scat, resembling black tapioca, and white markings on rocks from concentrated urine.

Pikas begin harvesting plants in mid-July, building stacks of a bushel or more; they later move them into dens deep within the rockpile. As Pikas remain active throughout the long alpine winter, this storehouse sustains them much of the year. One to two small litters of young are born each summer and are nurtured by both parents, who retreat to separate burrows in winter. Hawks, weasels, coyotes and martens prey on Pikas.

The name "Pika" derives from the Tunga people, Mongols from northern Siberia, and was originally pronounced *Peeka*. Other common names include Rock Rabbit, Piping Hare, Calling Hare, Little Chief Hare and Cony.

Indian Paintbrush
Lore and Luminosity

PRINKLED OVER THE WIDE WESTERN LANDSCAPE, FROM THE FLATLANDS OF Texas to the mountains of Montana, grow flower tufts the colors of fire and moonlight. Over arid deserts and plains, in wet mountain meadows and across cold alpine tundra, Indian Paintbrushes stand upright like lighted candles burning crimson and orange, rose and violet, yellow and cream. Folktales help connect man to nature and to the spirit world, and stories of the Indian Paintbrush typify those bonds.

Native Americans contribute two fables about this luminous wildflower. One legend suggests that the blossom's essence holds a potent love magic. Only scatter it over your sweetheart and amour will be everlasting. A second story tells of an Indian brave, artist for his tribe. Disappointed in his efforts to duplicate the colors of the sunset, he appealed to the Great Spirit. The artist's dedication was rewarded when the Great Spirit made him a gift of paintbrushes laden with the flaming hues of the evening sky. His picture completed, the brave tossed away his brushes which took root where they fell to bring the sunset to Earth.

An antiquated doctrine recommends that Indian Paintbrush be used to cool burning skin and to mitigate the sting of the centipede. Indian women were said to drink a mixture made from the plant's roots to dry up menstrual flow.

Castilleja, named for Spanish botanist Domingo Castillejo, is also called Painted-cup and Squaw Feather. Its flower spike resembles a ragged paintbrush laden with pigment. Color is concentrated in modified bracts while actual petals are green and inconspicuous. Plants are four to 16 inches tall with slender, often hairy, leaves. They grow in all climate zones of Colorado. Of the 200 species, most are native to the western United States; 24 species exist in the Rocky Mountains. Because paintbrushes hybridize, identification is often challenging. Some are parasitic, stealing nourishment from roots of nearby plants, especially sagebrush. A narrow-leaf, orange-red paintbrush is Wyoming's state flower.

Fireweed
Pyrotechnic Pioneer

AFTER LONDON WAS BOMBED AND BURNED IN WORLD WAR II, IT WAS RAPIDLY invaded. But this occupier brightened the mood of London's besieged residents. Ravaged city blocks, acres and acres of open space, metamorphosed into urban fields of flaming pink Fireweed—a vision unseen since Shakespeare's time. And only months after the infamous Yellowstone National Park forest fire, the charred earth was clothed in the exuberant beauty of Fireweed. This dazzler's common name derives from its habit of pioneering burn sites and its resemblance to flame.

As the first wildflower to colonize deforested land, thereby helping to stabilize the soil, Fireweed's spires grace moist, sunny locales disturbed by nature and by man. Roadside cuts through rich earth are prime candidates for spectacular Fireweed gardens. A superb reproductive system fosters this speedy incursion. Pods produce multitudes of tiny seeds, each tufted with long silky hairs that act as parachutes for easy distribution by the wind. Flowers arise from the ends of the pods, and the plant blooms from the bottom up, with individuals often exhibiting mature seed pods low on the stem, open blossoms at mid-stalk and buds at the top.

One-inch flowers, colored rose-pink, magenta or Oriental purple, have four petals and eight protruding stamens. They are arranged along an unbranched stalk two to three feet tall. Narrow lance-shaped leaves are two to six inches long. *Epilobium angustifolium* is widespread across the northern hemisphere with 100 species worldwide and 25 species in the Rockies. Its other common names are Blooming Sally, Great Willow-herb and Willowweed.

Plant parts were once harvested to treat asthma and whooping cough. Young leaves and shoots are edible after cooking, with the shoots eaten like asparagus. Mixing dried Fireweed leaves with tea leaves creates a flavorful new brew. Fireweed honey is deemed superior by the educated palate, and the plant is a favorite food of bears, deer and elk.

Look for erect spikes of Fireweed in the Maroon Bells region. In alpine tundra's wet places, scout for a dwarf species just a few inches tall. It bears fewer but larger blossoms and fleshy, wider leaves.

Furred and Feathered Feet

The pika, that fleet fur ball who cruises effortlessly over rock slides, is endowed with furred, skid-proof feet. That traction gives the nimble little speedster cocky confidence—even in confrontations with a deft predator like the bobcat.

The snowshoe hare has built-in equipment for winter wanderings over uncrusted white stuff. But the bigfoot bunny is not alone. Equally adept is the white-tailed ptarmigan, a high alpine grouse, whose heavily feathered legs and feet provide warmth in winter and allow easy walking atop fresh snow. Both the hare and ptarmigan have another nifty adaptation: They change to winter coats of pure white.

CASTLE CREEK

———— ⚌◈⚍ ————

The Ghost Town of Ashcroft
Stuart Mace
Castle Creek Hike
Wyoming Ground Squirrel
Pussytoes

CASTLE CREEK REGION

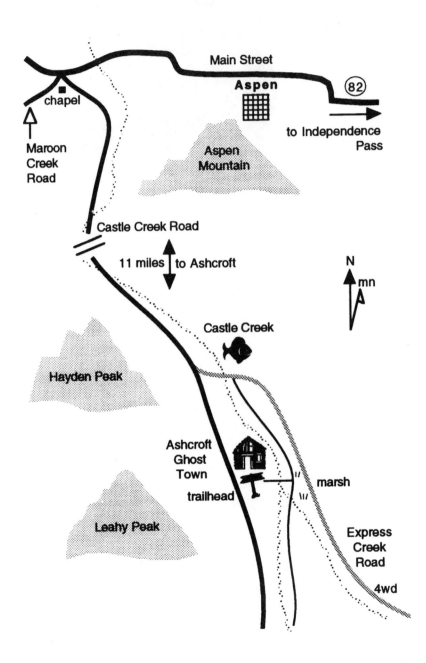

Main Street

Aspen

82

to Independence Pass

chapel

Maroon Creek Road

Aspen Mountain

Castle Creek Road

11 miles to Ashcroft

N
mn

Castle Creek

Hayden Peak

Ashcroft Ghost Town

trailhead

marsh

Leahy Peak

Express Creek Road

4wd

The Ghost Town of Ashcroft

WHEN HOPEFUL PROSPECTORS CROSSED INDEPENDENCE Pass in 1879, most staked claims on hillsides above the flat, alluvial bottomland that was to become Aspen. But Charles B. Culver and W.F. Coxhead ventured into the Castle Creek Valley where they too found silver. Highland mining camp evolved at midvalley, and soon, farther up the creek from Aspen, Castle Forks City was constituted. By 1880 Culver, other prospectors, and promoter Thomas E. Ashcraft (pronounced *Ashcroft*), had formed a Miner's Protective Association and laid out a townsite of 840 lots. The Castle Forks camp was renamed Chloride. Construction began on a harrowing toll road over Taylor Pass, linking Chloride and Aspen to Buena Vista and Leadville.

Even at 9500 feet above sea level, the new outpost crouched under sky-scraping peaks and lofty passes. Castle Peak, highest in the Elk Mountains at 14,265 feet, is nearby. Discovered and climbed by the Hayden Survey in 1873, the mountain was named for its towers, chimneys and pinnacles. Despite cold and avalanches, a handful of Chloride's settlers stayed the first winter.

By 1881 over 500 people occupied the mining camp, responding more to zealous promotion than to evidence of riches. In January of 1882 the town's name was officially changed to Ashcroft for the developer who had already departed the valley. In the spring, Jake Sands and the Fitzgerald brothers discovered rich silver deposits at 12,700 feet in a basin on the northeast side of Castle Peak. This lode in the Montezuma Mine sparked a silver rush, attracting both people and a legal squabble over the mine's ownership. Ashcroft, with its multiple routes over surrounding passes, was booming while Aspen was still struggling to produce ore and transport it to a processing site. A daily stage ran to Aspen, Independence and Leadville. Log cabins and pretentious false-fronted buildings grew apace. Irrigation ditches delivered water to every house.

By 1883 Ashcroft was larger than Aspen and led the region in silver production. The sterling Tam O'Shanter and Montezuma mines and two sawmills employed enough men to support two newspapers, six hotels and an indeterminate number of saloons and brothels. The town boasted a jail, a resident doctor and possibly a bowling alley. Early photographs show wooden sidewalks and several multi-storied buildings along the main street. One of those, a combination hotel-brothel still stands. Undocumented stories claim that the establishment's prostitutes were Spanish and that its cook was Chinese. The cook reportedly departed after an argument with the madam and founded the Yellow Boy Mine on what is now Yellow Boy Mountain. All of this is either unlikely or untrue, but legends persist. Perhaps 2000 people occupied the town at its zenith in 1884, but as early newspapers habitually inflated population numbers, the estimate may be high.

Yet Ashcroft was dead before the price of silver plummeted. Aspen had been the tortoise, appearing to lose to the hare. But when Aspen was at its height in 1892, Ashcroft counted between 250 and 500 residents. The rest had slipped away to the city on the Roaring Fork where major silver strikes, the arrival of two railroads and the milder climate at 7900 feet encouraged relocation. The railroads had bypassed Ashcroft and eliminated the arduous task of hauling Aspen's ore over mountain passes to Buena Vista and Crested Butte. Additionally, Ashcroft's low-grade ore and the expensive coke needed for the smelter did not justify the struggle with transportation. When the Montezuma Mine closed in 1920, upper valley life had become linked with the grazing of sheep and cattle. Postal service ceased in 1912 when about 50 people, mostly crusty old characters, called the place home.

A part-owner of Ashcroft's big mines was **Horace A.W. Tabor**, a Leadville silver magnate. Tabor, prosperous and well-connected in Washington, D.C., abandoned his respectable wife for an infamous romance with a young woman known as **Baby Doe.** The pair married, lived lavishly and lost everything when silver was demonetized. Baby Doe died alone and impoverished, frozen to death in a mining cabin at Tabor's once-precious Matchless Mine. It has become the stuff of legend and folk opera. Tabor Lake, an alpine gem accessed from Lincoln Creek Gulch, preserves the legendary name.

Though abandoned, Ashcroft's potential as a ski area attracted Billy Fiske and Ted Ryan in the 1930s. They invested in acreage, including some from colorful Jack Leahy—self-styled mayor, poet laureate and last of the original pioneers to leave Ashcroft. The new outdoorsmen built a ski lodge midvalley, but when Fiske was killed in World War II, Ryan leased the lodge to the 87th Mountain Infantry, a detachment of the 10th Mountain Division. The men arrived for winter ski training in 1942 before moving on to Camp Hale near Leadville and then to Italy. Later, Aspen eclipsed Ashcroft again as it became the premier downhill ski center of the Elk Mountains. Ted Ryan deeded the Ashcroft townsite to the U.S. Forest Service in 1953.

Today quiet Ashcroft is a destination for cross-country skiers, hikers and mountain bikers. Hikers access trails to American Lake, Cathedral Lake, Electric Pass, Hayden Peak and Castle Peak. Bikers challenge the uphills to Pearl and Taylor Passes. Many visitors pause at the Toklat Gallery. Almost everyone wanders through Ashcroft, passing by remnant buildings restored by the late Stuart Mace, the Aspen Historical Society, Pitkin County and the U.S. Forest Service. Cellar pits dug for food storage, nearby gooseberry bushes and clumps of rhubarb are more subtle remains of settlement. A summer caretaker, the "ghost" of Ashcroft, is available to answer questions and conducts walking tours daily, except Monday. The town is listed in the National Register of Historic Places, and while its human residents are long departed, the place bustles with the activity of Wyoming ground squirrels, cousins to the prairie dog.

Aspen to Destination: Drive or bicycle west on Route 82 from Mill and Main in Aspen. At 1.3 miles turn left at a traffic light onto Maroon Creek Road. Bear left immediately onto Castle Creek Road. The winding route carries you through a high valley rich with forest, creeks, beaver ponds, history, wildlife and an astonishing backdrop of snowy peaks. It is reason enough for a trip. Almost 10 miles from Route 82 is the handsome Elk Mountain Lodge and the trailhead for American Lake directly opposite.

Eleven miles from 82, signs indicate Toklat Gallery to the right and parking for the Ashcroft townsite across the road. A hitching post for bikes and a privy are in the parking lot. Two secluded picnic areas nestle in aspens and spruces next to Castle Creek. Bring your own water for drinking, and leave your dog at home and the flowers where they grow. The Castle Creek Trail begins at the end of Ashcroft's main street. Naturalist-guided walks originate at Toklat, the Mace family home and spiritual heart of the valley.

Stuart Mace
1919-1993

S TUART MACE, A BOTANIST AND A VETERAN 10TH MOUNTAINEER, RETURNED after World War II to the Castle Creek Valley, the wildly beautiful place he had known as a boy and as a serviceman. On an acre of land Mace and his wife Isabel built a home they named "Toklat"—an Eskimo word for the headwaters of a glacial mountain valley. Toklat would always be more than a place to raise five children. Whether lodge, restaurant, ecology center or gallery, it would reflect a union with the environment and with Earth's native peoples. And its resident family would become the conscience of the Aspen community, provoking dialogue about Man's compact with the Earth, locally and globally.

There are compelling reasons for calling Stuart Mace a guardian angel of the land. For it was his respect for the natural world, his tenacity in protecting it, and his eloquence in sharing his philosophy of responsible stewardship that earned him legendary status long before his death. Teaching by example, Mace balanced the unrecorded wisdom of the past with the scientific knowledge of the present. As an ecologist, educator and the resident sentinel of Castle Creek Valley, he saw all life as an interdependent whole, believing that humans may accept Earth's gifts only if they give back in equal measure. His spirit endures through his tangible legacy, through the continuing work of his family, and through the heightened sensitivities of all who knew him.

Ashcroft, the surrounding mountains, Stuart Mace and his sled dogs were featured in the 1950s television series **"Sergeant Preston of the Yukon."** Without prior experience, Mace volunteered to train dogsled teams as a 10th Mountaineer during World War II. A possible invasion of Norway prompted this preparation. Mace later bred and trained his own Malamutes and Siberian Huskies when he settled in the Castle Creek Valley. Four different canines played the part of "King," Preston's unflagging companion.

Descendents of Stuart Mace's dogs pull sleds during winter months from the Krabloonik Kennels in Snowmass Village.

Castle Creek Hike

GENERAL AREA:	Castle Creek Valley
TRAILHEAD:	12.3 miles from Mill & Main in Aspen
	15.7 miles from rodeo in Snowmass Village
HIKING DISTANCE:	1.0 to 2.0 miles
ELEVATION GAIN:	240 feet maximum
LOW POINT:	9400 feet at north branch terminus
HIGH POINT:	9640 feet at south branch terminus
HIGHLIGHTS:	Gentle footpath adjacent to Castle Creek
	A high montane valley below snowy peaks
	Ashcroft ghost town at trailhead
FISHING:	Rainbow trout in Castle Creek
NEARBY ATTRACTIONS:	Aspen!

Comments: This pleasant, easy walk along beautiful Castle Creek is appropriate for all ages and all fitness levels. It begins at Ashcroft ghost town in one of the loveliest and least-developed valleys in the region. The burbling creek, airy woods and flower-bedecked meadows give it a gentle, pastoral aspect. From Ashcroft the trail leads both north and south for a round trip of approximately one mile in each direction.

An alternative is to park short of the ghost town on Express Creek Road just beyond a bridge spanning Castle Creek. Do the complete two-mile walk with a midway visit to Ashcroft.

Aspen to Trailhead: Drive 1.3 miles west from Aspen on Route 82. At the traffic light, turn left onto Maroon Creek Road and bear left immediately onto Castle Creek Road. Continue up this special mountain valley for 11.0 miles to a parking area at left for Ashcroft ghost town. A map, historical marker and privy are in the parking lot. Watch carefully for bikers and runners on the road. Mule deer are often about in the very early morning.

Trail Route: The mid-trail starting point is opposite Hotel View—the two-story hotel-bordello at the end of Ashcroft's main street. The path heads directly into aspens and drops 30 feet to Castle Creek. Cross on a simple, sturdy bridge. From here you can turn right, walking south a half-mile and gaining 190 feet before the trail deadends at water's edge. Another choice is to bear left, walking north a half-mile and losing 50 feet of elevation before meeting Express Creek Road, an alternative trailhead.

South Path: The south, upvalley dirt trail advances into aspens, blue spruces and common junipers. The fragrant woods are light and bright, and Castle Creek is wonderfully musical. Step on rocks over a tributary and continue over conifer needles and mosses as you follow the meanderings of the creek. Five to 10 minutes into the walk bear left at a fork, moving slightly away from the water before rejoining it. The right spur also connects with the main trail but may be unsafe for young children as footing is tricky at the water's edge.

Just beyond this point is a pretty opening next to the creek. This is followed by a mild climb through aspens to a small meadow. Advance through a few more trees into a generous, sloping field high above the water. It is a beautiful viewspot with abundant wildflowers. At midsummer look for scarlet gilia, aspen daisy, sego lily, cinquefoil, umbrella plant, harebell, mountain goldenrod, pussytoes and yarrow. Conifers and willows grow here and there between the trail and creek.

Partway through this blooming field the trail descends gradually, ending at water's edge. Across the creek is a fence, Castle Creek Road and lofty Hayden Peak, named for the leader of a government survey team which mapped the area in the 1870s. Star Peak and Taylor Peak barricade the valley to the south.

Backtrack to the bridge below Ashcroft and either return to your vehicle or walk the level north leg of the trail.

North Path: Cross the bridge below Ashcroft and walk north along the right side of the creek for the trip to Express Creek Road. Immediately step over two tributaries on footbridges. Beavers are at work here, skillfully creating a pond and expanding the wetlands. Consequently, this trail description may be outdated. Look for pointed aspen stumps and felled trees. Many are huge. The magnitude of the beavers' undertaking is impressive. As you leave this burgeoning marsh and return to Castle Creek, there is a hitching post on the bank, and

Ashcroft is visible at left. In places where the path approaches the water, scout for the American Dipper/Water Ouzel (*Cinclus mexicanus*), a plump, gray songbird which nests along rushing water, trills merrily on midstream rocks, and dives and wades for its meals.

Move easily from aspens into small meadow and back into aspens. Much pale yellow northern paintbrush blooms aside the flowers seen on the southern path. On the right, dark tailings suggest a departed miner's efforts. Near a simple footbridge is a primitive cookstove and an old privy hidden in the trees, evidence of a more recent campsite.

From a broad open place you can see, across the creek, the Mace family's Toklat Gallery and an old cabin once occupied by Jack Leahy, an original occupant of Ashcroft. Leahy, famous locally as both the poet and mayor of Ashcroft, was the last old-timer to move away. The green mountain directly across the valley is named for him. The trail is a mix of dirt and paving as you approach Express Creek Road where a sign reads "Markley Hut, Barnard Hut, Goodwin-Greene Hut," all cross-country ski destinations. Another sign forbids camping here.

From this terminus, retrace your steps or walk Express Creek Road to Castle Creek Road, crossing a bridge en route. Bear left to return to Ashcroft, completing a small loop. On the return trip, walkers enjoy an uplifting view of snowy mountains at valley's end.

For more demanding hikes in the Castle Creek Valley, consult **The Aspen Dayhiker** for descriptions of the routes to American and Cathedral Lakes.

Wilderness: none   USGS map: Hayden Peak

Wyoming Ground Squirrel
Standing Tall

WESTERN PIONEERS TIED THEIR HORSES TO SHORT STAKES CALLED PICKET pins. When they encountered an engaging ground squirrel whose still, upright posture reminded them of the stakes, they named him "picket pin" as well. Today *Spermophilus elegans* is also known as the Wyoming Ground Squirrel.

While the Wyoming Ground Squirrel is similar in size to his silent Golden-mantled cousin, this alert, vocal resident warns of danger with a shrill whistle. His habit of snapping his tail as he pipes gives him another apt nickname, "Flickertail." The Golden-mantled Ground Squirrel maintains a tidy burrow entrance, but the Wyoming squirrel's doorway is piled with debris. And although the two species may inhabit neighboring grass or sagebrush montane meadows, the Golden-mantled squirrel alone is comfortable in forests and on alpine tundra.

Lacking the Golden-mantled's bold stripes, the Flickertail's coat seems homely. Gray, yellow-brown and faintly mottled, it blends with his terrain. Sitting erect, with front paws resting on his chest, he displays a whitish-buff belly. He prefers shortgrass territory where he feeds on insects, seeds and green vegetation, storing some in his burrow for the day he awakens from hibernation. Carrion also seems to be a dietary preference—even if the deceased was an acquaintance. An average of five or six young are born in May. Ground squirrels are quarry for coyotes, badgers, foxes, hawks, owls, weasels, bobcats and snakes.

Estivation: The Vanishing Act

Wherever did they go? Just last week the marmots and ground squirrels were frolicking near their burrows. But now, on this hot midsummer day, they are gone. No whistles, no flips of the tail, no curious stares. Nothing.

Some mammals, fish and reptiles husband energies by becoming summer sleepers. This temporary escape from prolonged heat and dryness is estivation, a summer counterpart of hibernation. Estivation is total with some animals: Their breathing and heartbeats slow and body temperatures drop, though not to the levels of hibernation; they cannot be awakened. Other animals rouse from time to time but remain in cool burrows; this is a retreat, not true estivation. While holed up, summer sleepers never drink or eat, as digestion generates warmth.

So those winsome marmots and ground squirrels are snoozing until the drought or hot spell ends. With a change in the weather, they'll be back to fatten up for winter's torpor. And at higher elevations, where refrigerated air and trickling snowmelt characterize summer, the furry critters are likely to remain astir and visible.

Wyoming Ground Squirrels are abundant in the ghost town of Ashcroft and on the dry, sunny slope behind Snowmass Village Center. Remain motionless and quiet, and these lively creatures will pop in and out of tunnels, busying themselves with affairs of the day.

Pussytoes
Fuzzy Confusion

The charming little wildflower known as Pussytoes has identity problems. It is decidedly not Pussypaws or Kittentails, each a different mountain flower. And while its longevity when dried contributed to the nickname Everlasting, it is not *Pearly* Everlasting, a related, but larger, plant. Pussytoes is its own small, soft self, unobtrusive in its many kindred species. A touch to its cluster of fuzzy, rayless flowerheads gives validity to its common name.

Other descriptive labels for this velvety blossom are Catspaw and Mouse Ear. The name of Ladies' Tobacco seems peculiar indeed, but perhaps it descends from Native Americans who chewed a gum made from the stalks of some species of western pussytoes. Europeans once packed the flowers among stored winter clothes to discourage moths and made them into a shampoo to combat lice, but it appears that no colorful names have descended from such practical uses. And the epithet Fur Balls has not been adopted even though the flowerhead resembles tiny balls of fur.

Three to eight white flowers comprise a one-inch cluster, each encircled by rows of translucent papery bracts—tinted white, rose, green or gray. Leaves are silvery green, woolly, lance-shaped and alternate on the stem; they form a rosette at the base. Most plants are two to 10 inches tall. They are found in varied microenvironments in Colorado from the foothills to the tundra. Precise identification of *Antennaria* is difficult as 20 similar species inhabit the Rocky Mountains, with about 12 in alpine areas. The rosy pussytoes of moist meadows and streambanks is especially pretty.

Pussytoes is usually mat-forming and grows in clumps apart from other plants. It releases a substance that discourages close neighbors, thus securing itself an adequate supply of water and nutrients. Some species have no male plants and reproduce without fertilization. Scout for the flowers in clearings along the Castle Creek Trail.

SNOWMASS VILLAGE

Snowmass Village
Snowmass Village Nature Trail
Ditch Trail Hike to East Snowmass Creek
Wildcat Rim Hike - North
Wildcat Rim Hike - SW
Black Bear
Western Serviceberry

SNOWMASS VILLAGE REGION

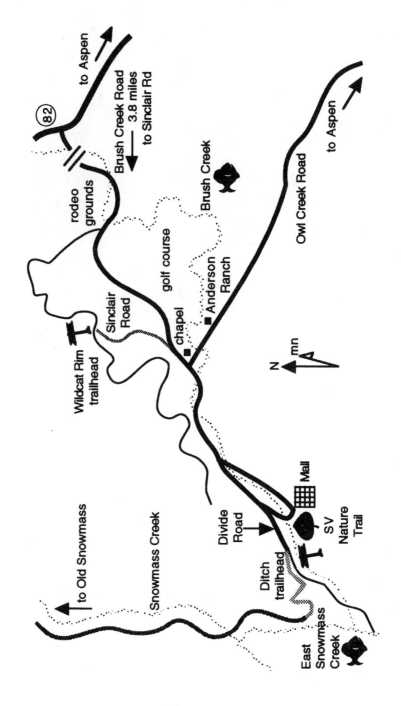

Snowmass Village
Artists and Cowboys, Ballerinas and Bears

Snowmass Village defies easy definition. In a sense, it is still putting its disparate pieces together to create a distinctive identity. Lacking Aspen's small town character, colorful history and Victorian architecture, Snowmass Village is, nonetheless, blessed with a breathtaking setting, proximity to nature and a plethora of possibilities. While this outdoorsy family resort is now a magnet for dancers and artists, it remains the home of cowboys and horses, elk and bears. And in that diversity lies its appeal.

While Aspen's fortunes rose and fell and rose again, the tiny community known as Brush Creek tended to sheep, cows and horses. The rich grassland and wildflower meadows of Brush Creek Valley sustained the livestock. Proximity to the Woody Creek train depot made the location ideal for cattle ranchers. So in 1894 the pioneer families built a one-room schoolhouse for their children, committing themselves to the land and to education. In use today as a preschool, it is one of several buildings recycled for modern purposes. And here and there, amidst sagebrush and yarrow, rest collapsing cabins and corroding tools. Some ranching continues in the lower valley, providing an authentic western tableau to anyone approaching Snowmass Village. And cowboy festivals plus a competitive weekly rodeo keep traditions alive.

This valley's water and abundant wildlife made it attractive to the Ute Indians long before whites entered the isolated Elk Mountains. An old story claims that the Utes set a forest fire in the 1870s to discourage venturesome settlers. Unwittingly, they may have cleared the land known as Big Burn for today's interlopers, the skiers.

In 1957 Bill Janss, a California developer and skier, saw resort potential in the Brush Creek Valley and subsequently purchased several local ranches. He also acquired a mountain permit from the U.S. Forest Service. So when Aspen's town fathers began to look for another skiing venue, Janss was poised to make an agreement. He did so in 1964, hoping to realize his vision of a complex of seven tiny villages connected by ski runs and chairlifts—a vision inspired by a European model. Fritz Benedict, who had also studied the terrain for its suitability for skiing, became the resort's master planner and architect. But Janss soon purchased the Sun Valley resort in Idaho, departing newborn Snowmass in 1967, the year of its debut. Financial considerations influenced construction of the first nodule, placing it close to ski runs on steep slopes at the head the valley. This site grew and grew, eclipsing Janss' idea of small, unique, interconnected villages.

But while Snowmass Village has matured into a major destination for skiers, it has also matured into a destination for artists. Seeds were planted in 1966 when ski resort developers invited ceramicist Paul Soldner to select one ranch on the acquired land as a place to nurture artisans and their students. The Anderson family's sheep ranch is today's Anderson Ranch Arts Center, its original log barns augmented by new, suitably rustic studios and residences. A summer ballet school followed, with classes and rehearsals held in outdoor locations. The Aspen Music Festival expanded, scheduling free classical performances in the village. Summer visitors may also attend dance and art lectures and outdoor pop music concerts, all free of charge. A new cultural focus is American music: jazz, blues, gospel.

An extensive Village trail system is expanding, allowing walkers, runners and cyclists access to many interconnecting miles of valley, ridge and mountainside. Two routes, Government Trail and Owl Creek Trail, already link Snowmass and Aspen. Some paved paths, just steps from most lodging units, lead to woodsy, dirt hiking trails where wildlife holes up when not out and about in local neighborhoods. The line between civilization and nature is pleasantly vague here.

As Snowmass Village continues to redefine itself, additional recreational opportunities will tempt visitors to explore the area's exquisite outdoors. Ask questions, gather your gear and sally forth.

Snowmass Village Nature Trail

T HE SNOWMASS VILLAGE NATURE TRAIL PROVIDES A LEISURELY OUTDOOR
excursion for every family member. It serves as a good introduction
to the flora of the Rockies' montane zone and as a gentle first step
toward acclimating to hills and high altitude. Gaining 280 feet of elevation,
the narrow path winds upward for about one mile. The trail begins behind
the bus terminal adjacent to the upper level of the Snowmass Village Mall.
A map for a self-guided tour is available at the mall's information booth, and
a walk led by a naturalist begins at 10 a.m. Monday through Friday. Meet
at the booth. Both the map and guided walk are free.

Look for a green "Nature Trail" sign and for steps built from railroad ties.
The path ascends through wooded land near Brush Creek left of Divide
Road. Numbered markers relate to information on the printed guide. At
station number 14, for example, the guide reads, "Look for the cluster of
flowerless green plants called Horsetail. Horsetail are very primitive
plants.... Millions of years ago when moist and warm climate conditions
existed ... horsetail grew to the size of giant sequoia trees."

You pass among wildflowers, trees and tall grasses, cross a meadow and
approach a small cascade in the creek. Children will like this watery spot
for play, but do not let them drink the water or lick wet fingers. Microscopic
giardia, an intestinal parasite, inhabits most streams. Also, watch out for
posts with attached barbed wire—like the cabin ahead, remnants of
ranching days.

Picnic tables offer a place to pause, and a nearby footbridge over the creek
leads to the old cabin. The path ahead has a few short steep sections, but
a relaxing pace is appropriate here. At station 18 the trail's end is visible.
Post 19 marks the terminus and takes you to a Nature Trail sign at the top
and to a wide dirt road, known as the Sleighride Trail, that returns you to
the Village by a different route.

When the Hayden Survey team mapped the Elk Mountains in 1873 and 1874, Henry Gannett, the group's topographer, broke from his habit of naming peaks for their appearance when he awarded the moniker of Augustus Daly to a square-topped mass with a distinctive diagonal band. Adjacent to aptly christened Capitol Peak, **Mount Daly** honored that era's president of the American Geological Society. Today the striped sentinal hovers over Snowmass Village and the Brush Creek Valley.

For a beautiful view of Mount Daly and Snowmass Creek Valley, walk a short distance up the dirt road to a high point called The Divide. For a more vigorous outing, continue on the Ditch Trail to East Snowmass Creek.

Aspen to Destination: Take an RFTA bus to Snowmass Village or drive west on Route 82. If you drive, turn left at 6.0 miles from Mill and Main in Aspen and follow winding Brush Creek Road for more than five miles uphill to the Village Mall. Signs direct visitors to parking areas.

Ditch Trail Hike to East Snowmass Creek

GENERAL AREA:	Snowmass Village
TRAILHEAD:	12.1 miles from Mill & Main in Aspen
	3.4 miles from rodeo in Snowmass Village
HIKING DISTANCE:	3.8 miles round trip from the Divide
ELEVATION GAIN:	160 feet
LOW POINT:	8920 at trailhead
HIGH POINT:	9080 feet at East Snowmass Creek
HIGHLIGHTS:	Water, expansive views and wild berries
FISHING:	Rainbow trout in East Snowmass Creek
NEARBY ATTRACTIONS:	Snowmass Village Nature Trail
	Rodeo and free weekly outdoor concerts
	Village boutiques and restaurants

Comments: This hike to East Snowmass Creek may be an extension of either the woodsy Snowmass Village Nature Trail or the Sleighride Trail, a dirt road accessed at the top of Snowmelt Road. It may also be started from the Divide, a high point above the Village. From the Divide, the excursion is a gentle hike over undulating terrain and offers splendid views of Mount Daly, a waterfall and Snowmass Creek Valley. The trail crosses over ski runs transformed by summer into flowery meadows; it parallels Brush Creek irrigation ditch through light woods to bustling East Snowmass Creek.

Aspen to Trailhead: If you are continuing from the Nature Trail, bear right at a dirt road known as the Sleighride Trail and walk ahead to a stone marker for "The Divide." Cross the parking area and move into the woods where a sign says "Campground Lift 5."

From Aspen, drive 6.0 miles west on Route 82 from Mill and Main. Signs at a traffic light direct you to turn left onto Brush Creek Road to reach Snowmass Village. Remain on winding, scenic Brush Creek Road through open ranch land, past the rodeo grounds and golf course, under a wooden bridge and ahead through an intersection near a small business center. A half-mile beyond the wooden bridge, stay right and follow Divide Road for another 0.9 miles uphill. Bear left at a blue sign for "Base Lot E." A stone marker reads "The Divide." Drive into a parking area past a handsome stone and wood building fronted by a pond. At the lot's end, a sign for "Campground Lift 5" marks the trailhead.

Trail Route: Walk into aspens and firs on a 4WD road. The level track narrows as it bisects a steep meadow, which is a ski run in the winter. Ahead is Mount Daly, the symbolic guardian of Snowmass Village. Down to the right is Snowmass Creek Valley and beyond are the furrowed Woody Creek hills. The views are lovely here. At meadow's end is an irrigation ditch diverting water from East Snowmass Creek. A tiny waterfall splashes down from the left, trickling under the trail. Much soft, green horsetail grows in the wetness, and leafy thimbleberry plants exhibit big white blossoms in June and July and large, edible, raspberry-like fruits in August.

Cross another ski trail which resembles a sloping meadow. Far across the valley is a gravel road which is the wilderness access road from old Snowmass. The track you walk again widens as it melds with dirt road from below. On your return, remember to stay on the high side when you approach this fork. A chair lift signals that you are indeed in ski country.

The footpath becomes a bit rocky and narrows again along the irrigation ditch. The soil's color changes to red, indicating the presence of iron oxide. Soon the view is spacious, and the trail broadens and bends to the left. Before you is a waterfall plunging toward Snowmass Creek. Your goal is a tributary, East Snowmass Creek.

Walk a gentle uphill, and then drop into aspens and then into spruces and firs. The red path winds a bit as it descends, and the creek is soon audible. The trail levels out in a pretty aspen grove brightened by orange paintbrush and tall blue penstemon. The ditch is to your right beyond a grassy area that hides wild strawberries. The ditch is a safe place for small children to dabble in the water while the creek ahead may be a torrent in a big snow year. Never, however, allow children to drink any untreated water or to lick wet fingers. Giardia can be the miserable result.

Hefty red boulders rest in the grasses. Look for a big fir tree with two neighboring boulders at the trail's right edge. Just beyond is a blue spruce. At the spruce, step over the ditch to the trail's right to view the main creek below. In early summer it is full and noisy. Take an immediate right onto a path after crossing the ditch; wind down to the bank of East Snowmass Creek, avoiding the steep direct route. This is a place to pause or picnic.

Remember when backtracking to stay right when you approach a fork. Take the high narrow path, not the low wide road.

From the parking area there are three routes back to the Snowmass Village Mall: via automobile and Divide Road; by foot on the daisy-edged, dirt and gravel road called Sleighride Trail to the top of Snowmelt Road; and by foot on the Nature Trail, which branches left from the dirt road.

Hike Extension: Across East Snowmass Creek is a short sidetrail that connects with the main East Snowmass Trail to East Snowmass Pass and Willow Lake. It is a long uphill journey to the pass, but lovely meadows and mountain splendor may be found just a few miles up the East Snowmass Creek Valley. If the water flow in the creek is low, you can cross to explore this uncrowded region.

For two demanding hikes from Snowmass Village, consult The **Aspen Dayhiker** for trail descriptions to Snowmass Lake and Pierre Lakes.

Wilderness: none   USGS map: Highland Peak

Wildcat Rim Trail
The Options

THIS VIEW TRAIL MEANDERS ATOP A NARROW, SERPENTINE RIDGE DIVIDING Snowmass Village from the valley to the northwest. The trail dips and rises as it delivers a scenic feast of both the Brush Creek Valley and the Maroon Bells-Snowmass Wilderness peaks beyond. Wildflowers are lovely, small butterflies flit everywhere, mountain bluebirds flaunt sky-blue feathers, grasshoppers pop about noisily, chipmunks chatter in the brush and signs of larger creatures abound. As the Rim is an arid place of shrubs and few shade trees, the hike is best undertaken in the morning or evening when breezes are cool and the sun is low. Serious hiking boots are not necessary, but the athletic shoes chosen must have cleated soles designed for traction on some steep, gravelly grades along the topside. Water is essential. As the trail sometimes winds close to cliff edges and is bordered in spots by barbed wire fencing, this is not a trip for impetuous children.

The Wildcat Rim Trail offers options to everyone from sluggish scenery buffs to energetic fitness nuts. Choose your starting and ending points based on your personal desire for exercise. Sweeping views characterize the entire route.

This guide divides the Rim Trail into two segments—North and Southwest. Each may be accessed from a parking area at the top of Sinclair Road. Walk until satisfied and return to your vehicle. The north section may also be an uphill-downhill loop, requiring more time, stamina and fluids. Read the separate hike descriptions for details.

Wildcat Rim Hike - North
Lower Snowmass Village

GENERAL AREA:	Snowmass Village
SR TRAILHEAD:	11.1 miles from Mill & Main in Aspen
HR TRAILHEAD:	8.7 miles from Mill & Main in Aspen
HIKING DISTANCE:	up to 4.0 miles for topside round trip
	6.0 miles for complete loop
ELEVATION GAIN:	460 feet from Sinclair Road
	1100 feet from Horse Ranch near rodeo
LOW POINT:	8520 feet at Sinclair Road trailhead
	7880 feet at Horse Ranch trailhead
HIGH POINT:	8980 feet on Rim
HIGHLIGHTS:	Panorama of wilderness and Village
	Mountaintop feeling at moderate altitude
	Serenity within sight of development
FISHING:	None on trail; brook trout in Brush Creek
NEARBY ATTRACTIONS:	Snowmass Village Nature Trail
	Rodeo and free weekly outdoor concerts
	Village boutiques and restaurants

Comments: The north leg of the Wildcat Rim overlooks lower Snowmass Village and the vast Wildcat Ranch on the Rim's opposite side. Its spacious views include the splendor of the nearby mountain wilderness. While this trail's topside terrain makes it less challenging than the southwest section, it is occasionally vague as it is crossed by horse paths, overgrown in places and broken by erosion and small gullies. For the easiest excursion, drive to the top of Sinclair Road, walk north and return to your vehicle.

For a substantial hike with a higher level of difficulty, make a loop by climbing steeply up to the Rim from the Horse Ranch trailhead, walk the Rim one-way, descend to the valley via Sinclair Road and return to your start using the paved Brush Creek Trail alongside Brush Creek Road. Another option is to plant a car at the top of Sinclair Road before starting at the Horse Ranch trailhead.

Aspen to Sinclair Trailhead: From Aspen, drive 6.0 miles west on Route 82 from Mill and Main. At the traffic light, signs direct you left onto Brush Creek Road to Snowmass Village. Remain on Brush Creek Road for 3.8 miles as it weaves past open ranch land, the rodeo grounds and much of the golf course. Turn right onto Sinclair Road opposite the blue-roofed Snowmass Villas condominiums positioned between the road and golf course. Drive 1.3 miles up the winding residential street until it ends at the crest of the ridge that encloses Snowmass Village to the west. Park at right near a yellow "Rim Trail" sign. Here is the access point for a walk along the ridgetop in a northerly direction. Behind you is an identical sign designating a continuation of the trail as it heads southwest.

A nearby marker, a closed gate and low red stone pillars announce the entrance to the private Wildcat Ranch. The Rim Trail edges the ranch property.

Horse Ranch Trailhead: As of 1995, this alternate access route is under development. Intended for hikers and mountain bikers only, the trail should be cleared, though signage may be lacking. Park at the rodeo grounds, 2.7 miles from Route 82. Walk a paved path alongside Horse Ranch entry road. The path becomes gravel, passes a small building at right, and ends at a cul-du-sac. Scout ahead for signs of a trail. Then hike uphill toward the ridgetop and walk the Rim in a southwest direction.

Trail Route: From Sinclair Road climb a path to the right alongside a wooden fence demarcating the Wildcat Ranch land. Purple lupine carpets this slope and much of the route in June and early July. At the top of the small rise is another sign identifying the Rim Trail. No use is permitted from September 15 until June 1 as this is a critical wildlife movement period. Dogs are not welcome on the trail because of wildlife and horses, but if you must bring your pet, make certain it is leashed. The sign instructs hikers and mountain bikers to use the routes marked in blue; horses and their riders are to follow the red markers.

The red and blue trail markers were not in place as of 1994, but the meandering footpath ahead is obvious. Always stay right of the ranch fence as you walk. The Rim abounds in eroded surfaces. Should the trail approach a small gully, scout for a way around it. In several such cases, the best plan is to bear left.

To begin, walk above the golf course and the Melton Ranch and Wild Oak subdivisions. The already expansive vista will improve dramatically as you advance. The trail has a rolling quality as it rises and falls. In a few minutes you stand above the Horse Ranch subdivision on the right and the Wildcat Reservoir on the left. As you gain elevation along the ridge via several short, sharp uphills, the snowy peaks of the Maroon Bells-Snowmass Wilderness emerge from behind nearby hills. Clark Peak, Capitol Peak, Mount Daly and Mount Sopris, connected by an extended ridge to the right of the others, add visual pleasure on a monumental scale. In the opposite direction are the mountains of the Holy Cross Wilderness.

But abundant small pleasures abound. Look for flashes of blue as mountain bluebirds swoop from trees to snatch low-flying insects. Their rare color makes them easy to spot. Myriad butterflies flutter about, and animal tracks are left everywhere in the dirt trail. This is a quiet, tranquil place where the only sounds are those of birds and insects.

Gambel oaks are the local trees, and serviceberry, mountain mahogany and big sagebrush add bushy greenery. But the vivid, specialized flowers in this dry exposed place truly delight the eye. Spring blossoms are arrowleaf balsamroot and wild roses. By mid-June there are carpets of golden mule ears and purple lupine; pink and scarlet fairy trumpets, orange paintbrush and gold cinquefoil are dotted about. July is characterized by bountiful bright yellow sulphurflowers; white ballhead sandwort, the sophisticated white sego lily and lilac aspen daisies grow nearby. In August the daisies are joined by golden rabbitbrush for an exuberant show.

Ahead, the ridge wraps to the right where, atop a green-clothed hillside, is a narrow radio tower. This portion of the Rim trail moves toward that spot but ends some distance from it. The wire fence that marked the boundary of Wildcat Ranch is replaced by yellow posts with a "no trespassing" message. Stay to the right of these yellow markers as the trail remains quite close to the boundary. From here until the turnaround point, numerous sidetrails drop downhill to the right. Most are made by wild animals or horses, and many will interconnect and eventually lead back to Horse Ranch and the rodeo grounds.

As you reach a high point, a yellow post stands at mid-trail and logs lie across the path. To the left is a very green, very pointed hill. To continue, bear right and downhill into aspens, shrubs, tall grasses and flowers. In this wetter place, fragrant blue Colorado columbines bloom in early summer. The yellow ranch boundary markers are not visible here, but after about five minutes, you emerge into the open where the posts again confirm your route.

As you move forward, look left for a shallow, muddy pond tucked against some aspens in a small, low meadow. Pass briefly through an overgrown section of trail and ascend a small rise onto a broad, open, grassy knoll. Ahead are twin rounded hillsides. They seem a natural blockade. The radio tower tops the mound to the right. Close below the Rim on the right is another pond. This knoll is a good turnaround point as the trail disappears in the grass here. It is a place to pause and take in the awesome 360-degree panorama. This is camera country.

Retracing your steps rewards you with the vista of wilderness mountains. Keep the Wildcat Ranch property markers on your right as you walk. The undulating trail is conspicuous ahead. In the few places where the trail forks, bear right to avoid awkward footing in small gullies.

This round trip can take anywhere from 80 minutes to over two hours with the time depending entirely upon your pace and pauses.

Wilderness: none   USGS map: Highland Peak

Wildcat Rim Hike - SW

Upper Snowmass Village

GENERAL AREA:	Snowmass Village
TRAILHEAD:	11.1 miles from Mill & Main in Aspen
HIKING DISTANCE:	up to 4.6 miles for topside round trip
ELEVATION GAIN:	480 feet
LOW POINT:	8520 feet at Sinclair Road trailhead
HIGH POINT:	9000 feet on Rim
HIGHLIGHTS:	Panorama of wilderness and Village
	Mountaintop feeling at moderate altitude
	Serenity within sight of development
FISHING:	None on trail; brook trout in Brush Creek
NEARBY ATTRACTIONS:	Snowmass Village Nature Trail
	Rodeo and free weekly outdoor concerts
	Village boutiques and restaurants

Comments: The southwest section of the Wildcat Rim overlooks mid and upper Snowmass Village and the vast Wildcat Ranch on the Rim's opposite side. Its views include the splendor of the nearby mountain wilderness. While this leg of the Rim trail is well-worn and easy to follow, it has more abrupt, gravelly ups and downs than the north leg. The Village has plans for switchbacks in the steepest sections. To access the trail, drive to the top of Sinclair Road; walk southwest and return to your vehicle. (A loop may eventually be possible with development of a second trailhead near the Mountain View condominiums.)

Aspen to Trailhead: See Wildcat Rim - North for directions to the Sinclair Trailhead. At the top of Sinclair Road, a yellow "Rim Trail" sign to the left marks the access point for a walk along the ridgetop in a southwest direction. Next to the Wildcat Ranch gate is an identical sign designating a continuation of the trail as it heads north.

Trail Route: From Sinclair Road walk uphill through fragrant sagebrush, orange paintbrush and lilac aspen daisies. Purple lupine and golden mule ears are everywhere in early July. A few yards from the start is another yellow "Rim Trail" sign, also mounted on a redwood post. The wire fence to the trail's right is topped by a barbed span. Do not grab for it on steep sections. The trail flattens amidst oak trees and sulphurflowers. Two houses perch on a prominence to the west, but all other buildings are far below in Snowmass Village. The trail begins above the Melton Ranch subdivision.

Ascend on gravelly soil. Cleated soles are helpful here. At the top of the rise is the beautiful vision of Clark Peak, Capitol Peak and Mount Daly, standing left to right. The sights are unobstructed from this high ridge which plummets into the Village on the left and drops less sharply on the right into the quiet, green valley of Wildcat Ranch. The fence is now on your left. Its position will change many times throughout the hike. Occasional yellow Wildcat Ranch posts warn of trespassing.

The trail resembles a roller coaster as it lifts and falls, levels out and turns sharply at viewspot corners. Some slopes are very steep. The ski area mountain is ahead with the bigger, often snowy, peaks to its right. There is a mix of Douglas-firs, aspens and sagebrush. Mountain mahogany, Rocky Mountain maple and serviceberry are shrub-size. With the sun behind you in the early morning, the valley and mountains ahead are beautifully illuminated. This lofty place catches a breeze, and despite the Village vista, seems miles from anywhere. Its quiet is broken only by the soft sounds of whirring hummingbirds, tapping woodpeckers and popping grasshoppers. Mountain bluebirds swoop from fenceposts, and chipmunks talk in the brush.

At the crest of a tough uphill you can locate Wildcat Reservoir on the right. Beyond, make a sharp climb through Douglas-firs and white firs, Rocky Mountain and common junipers. Where the path flattens again, the space is broad, less ridge-like.

The next viewpoint is a perpendicular dropoff over the mid-Village area, locale of Snowmass Center businesses, the post office, Anderson Ranch, the chapel and fire station. Here the trail makes an abrupt right turn and then runs just below the spine of the ridge to the Wildcat Ranch side.

Across a sagebrush meadow you see Mount Sopris to the west. As you advance, the scene of Sopris is lost, but the Mountain View condominiums appear below, just across Brush Creek from the Village Mall. The topside trail is gentle through here, and then, as it ascends once more, you begin to spot the houses of The Divide above Snowmass Village.

The path traverses another flat sagebrush meadow before passing between aspens. It climbs to a point from which shallow Zeigler Lake is visible below to the left. The trail terminates at a private road just beyond a sharp right turn along a fence.

Everywhere on this aerial excursion, it is easy to determine where you are in relation to landmarks. The two ridgeline houses at the hike's beginning, for example, are conspicuous reference points. The Village buildings provide regular feedback. There is no mystery or confusion about this route as it shadows the twisting Rim.

On the return trip the ridgeline houses grow steadily larger. Beyond are the furrowed hills above Woody Creek. At the dropoff viewpoint above mid-Village, you are almost halfway back to the start from the turnaround at the private dirt road. The precipitate downhills encountered in this direction require careful placement of feet and occasional braking action. Proposed switchbacks will mitigate the steepness.

A steady, moderate pace to the trail's end results in a round trip of about two and a half hours. Fast walkers may do this in two hours, while many people may take a relaxing journey of three hours or more.

Wilderness: none   USGS map: Highland Peak

Black Bear
Not Exactly Teddy

THEY PEER IN WINDOWS, NOSES PRESSED AGAINST THE GLASS. THEY RAID BIRD feeders on porches and decks, punch through screens at midday to pillage meat thawing in kitchens, push open unlocked doors to gorge on jumbo bags of dog food, saunter through condominium complexes and window-shop on the Snowmass Village Mall.

Bears. The residents of Snowmass Village know a lot about bears. While sightings are reported to Village police almost daily during warm months, many chance meetings are private moments, never placed on record. Of course, bears are out and about in urbane Aspen as well: swimming at midnight in the Ritz Carlton pool, soaking in a private hot tub, breaking down a garage door to ransack trash containers, plundering dumpsters. But it is Snowmass Village that begets the most bear stories each summer. A local ordinance now punishes residents who fail to place their garbage in bear-proof containers. Untempted by man's leavings, bears remain in their normal habitat. Tempted, they can become dangerous pests who must be relocated or killed.

Colorado has approximately 12,000 Black Bears, the smallest and most widespread of North America's wild bears. But this solitary, powerful native is neither petite nor always black. Bears may weigh 200 to 500 pounds, stand 2.0 to 3.5 feet at the shoulder and measure 4.5 to 6.0 feet in length. Erect, they may leave claw marks nine feet up a tree trunk. And while in the East, Black Bears are black, in the mountains of the West their dense fur may be black, chestnut or cinnamon. Muzzles are tan and breasts often wear white blazes.

All bear species have small, somewhat rounded ears, little eyes set close together and short tails lost in fur. But *Ursus americanus* sports a straight "Roman nose" while the Grizzly's profile is concave. Bears walk much like humans with the entire sole touching the earth. On wet ground they leave broad prints with five toes and five claw marks. While their shuffling, flatfooted gait may appear clumsy, bears can break into a rolling run of 30 m.p.h. for short distances. They are also strong swimmers and tree-climbers. Bears have poor eyesight, average hearing and an excellent sense of smell.

Though primarily nocturnal, bears may be glimpsed at any hour as they forage for food over a territory of eight to 15 square miles. True omnivores, they eat almost anything. In autumn, bears may feed 20 hours a day to lay on enough fat for a long winter's dormancy—a period of light sleep when their body temperatures drop only a few degrees below normal. After denning up for the harshest months in or under any natural shelter—cave, crevice, hollow log, rock pile, downed tree or snow—bears emerge thin and disheveled in their molting winter coats.

Every other spring many females are accompanied by one to three cubs born in January or February. Only seven to 12 ounces at birth, the cubs have much growing to do. They often remain with their mother, a protective and strict guardian, for a year. Bears are sexually mature at age three and may live 30 years. A 1992 Colorado law outlaws bear baiting by hunters and eliminates the spring hunt so that lactating sows will not be killed, thus dooming their cubs.

Bears leave more than big footprints in the woods. Trees with rough bark may show rub marks or snagged fur where the animals try to relieve itches and to rid themselves of loose hair. Other trees exhibit scars from teeth and claws. But while these signs and actual sightings are fascinating, bears are still wild creatures; they can be formidable if they have cubs and if they are surprised, hungry, injured, feeding, breeding or guarding kill.

Should you meet a Black Bear while hiking, stay calm. If he has not seen you, walk away from the area while speaking aloud to alert him to your presence. He does not want to confront you. If you come face to face, back away slowly, speak softly, avoid eye contact and make a wide detour to give him room to escape. Never run or make sudden movements. As each bear encounter is different, there is no perfect behavioral formula. Evaluate carefully and adjust to the situation. Remember, you are the visitor.

Western Serviceberry
An August Edible

THEY DANGLE FROM LONG STALKS IN BLACKISH PURPLE CLUSTERS, OFFERING themselves as instant energy capsules to flagging hikers. Sweet and juicy when ripe, the Western Serviceberry is ready-made trail food.

Across North America, Native Americans and early explorers valued the versatile serviceberry. Native Americans may have invented the first portable energy bar when they preserved the fruit for winter by drying crushed berries and compressing them into cakes. Dried berries were also combined with dried meat pounded to a paste and with animal fat to make pemmican, a complete meal in handy cake form. Berries, dried like raisins or currants, may be stewed or cooked with various meats. And a fresh harvest is excellent for pies, pancakes, muffins, conserves, jelly and wine.

Western Serviceberry occurs as a shrub or small tree, usually growing in clumps. It has several trunks and a narrow, rounded crown. Widespread in Colorado, its range may extend to 10,000 feet of elevation. *Amelanchier alnifolia* is common on brushy, rocky hillsides where it grows among gamble oak, mountain mahogany, chokecherry and sagebrush. The bush is also found with aspen and along creeks and rivers.

Serviceberry's small green leaves are rounded with jagged teeth near the tip; undersides are lighter in color and slightly hairy. Loose hanging clusters of white, star-shaped, one-inch flowers make the shrub showy and fragrant in the spring. Berries are first red, then purple-black when ripe; one-quarter to one-half inch in diameter, they have five tiny, toothlike projections similar to a blueberry or a miniature apple. As fruit quality varies, taste tests are recommended. Serviceberry, also known as Saskatoon, Western Shadbush and Juneberry, is a favorite of birds, squirrels and bears. It matures in late summer at high elevations.

Scout for serviceberry bushes within Snowmass Village and along the Rim Trail, the Sunnyside Trail, the Shadow-Aspen Mountain Loop and the Hunter Creek Trail.

MIDWAY

Independence Toll Road
The Grottos
The Roaring Fork Braille Trail
Weller Lake Hike
Midway Pond Hike
Golden-Mantled Ground Squirrel
Lost Man Reservoir

MIDWAY REGION

N
mn

to Aspen

Williams Mountains

to Midway Pass

Midway Pond

Peak 13033

marsh

Lost Man Creek

Lost Man Reservoir

trailhead

Roaring Fork River

Green Mountain

Braille Trail

82

Lincoln Creek Road

Grottos

trailhead

Weller Lake

to Independence Pass

Independence Toll Road

THE MIDWAY REGION WAS ONCE DISTINGUISHED BY A STAGECOACH STOP located midway between Aspen and Independence Pass. Weller Stage Station was built in 1882 near the confluence of Lincoln Creek and the Roaring Fork River. The Weller name seems to descend from the station keeper. The building housed 60 to 70 people, but these overnight guests could expect little more than a pallet on the floor. Bunks were reserved for changing shifts of stage drivers and their armed companions, known as express messengers.

The station sat by a crude toll road that traversed Independence Pass from Aspen to Leadville. The route followed a prospector's trail and was constructed in 1881 by B. Clark Wheeler for $10,000—an expenditure equal to 1.5 million dollars in 1993. Typical fees ranged from one dollar for a horseback rider to five dollars for a four-horse team. Some travelers paid the Carson Brothers Stage Line to ferry them over the pass.

Stagecoaches, even the finely built Concord coaches, shoehorned nine passengers and excess cargo into an area so cramped that travelers sat hip to hip on their allotted seat space of 15 inches (two inches less than airline economy seats today). Their knees rapped against those of their three hapless fellows positioned on a backless center bench. This trio clung to leather loops suspended from the ceiling as the vehicle heaved and rocked like a storm-tossed ship. Leg space may have been assigned to bulging sacks that would not fit elsewhere. Leather pouches stuffed with mail and an iron strongbox of valuables were stowed in a front "boot" under the driver's seat; express packages and travelers' baggage went into the coach's back boot; extra bundles or desperate passengers might ride on the roof. Leather curtains on open windows were inadequate against dust, cold and driving rain.

On lengthy journeys through the West, "stage-craziness" was a recognized malady. People went berserk from the crowding, the violent motion of the speeding coach, the unspeakable filth, the absence of bathing facilities, the inedible food, and the peril from ungraded roads, swollen rivers, blinding blizzards, angry Indians and opportunistic bandits. Worst of all was lack of sleep. On long cross-country trips, coaches paused only to change horses or drivers. Nothing less than a serious emergency would force an overnight delay. Travelers were expected to slumber while sitting upright in the jouncing box. Sometimes fatigue led to fatal friction between passengers.

An 1877 column in the *Omaha Herald* provided tips to the traveler: "The best seat inside a stage coach is the one next to the driver. You will have to ride with back to the horses, which with some people, produces an illness not unlike sea sickness, but ... you will get more rest, with less than half the bumps and jars than on any other seat.... If a team runs away, sit still and take your chances; if you jump, nine times out of ten you will be hurt. In very cold weather abstain entirely from liquor ... a man will freeze twice as quick while under its influence.... Don't smoke a strong pipe inside especially early in the morning; spit on the leeward side of the coach.... Don't swear, nor lop over on your neighbor when sleeping.... Don't discuss politics or religion, nor point out places on the road where horrible murders have been committed, if delicate women are among the passengers.... Don't imagine for a moment you are going on a pic-nic...."

The Independence Toll Road was a typical route through the Rocky Mountains. Coaches and wagons bumped along a narrow shelf carved into precipitous rock walls. A stage was driven as fast as the horses could draw it, sweeping around a curve with nothing visible ahead except sky. Again and again, a vehicle seemed to swing over an abyss and then back toward a rock face. Lead horses vanished as the road snaked around corners. Most drivers were experts, speaking to their teams through subtle use of the reins. One traveler described a driver as "a skilled musician playing upon a familiar instrument." With sharp inclines, tree stumps, boulders, potholes and deep mud obstructing passage, the Independence Pass journey was always memorable. Passengers regarded this either as an adventure or a nightmare. In winter, coach wheels were replaced by runners, creating bulky, enclosed sleds. Riders resembled shapeless, faceless bundles in the frigid temperatures.

A portion of the old toll road may be walked today at the Grottos where broad granite rocks wear scars from the wheels of wagons and stagecoaches.

The Grottos

A POPULAR STOPPING PLACE IN THE MIDWAY AREA, THE GROTTOS IS celebrated for its cascades, ice caves, swirling water, smooth granite formations, sandy beach and natural wading pools. The Roaring Fork River created the Grottos and continues to sculpt it today. There are diversions here for families and photographers, for the active and the sedentary. Careful supervision of children is necessary near wild water, ice caverns and stacked boulders. Fly fishermen can find quiet retreats upriver from the main attractions.

In the parking area, Forest Service signs provide a topographical map and a brief lesson in botany. Elevation here is 9560 feet. An attractive pictorial map of the Grottos stands just before a wooden bridge over the Roaring Fork. This overview is helpful in planning your excursion. Note that there is both an outer loop for walkers and a small inner loop designated as wheelchair accessible. The trails are not paved, and the wheelchair route is fairly rough in spots. But the voice of the river, the perfume of the pines, and the vision of shattered, towering rock faces make this a wonderful destination.

Cross the bridge to begin your loop walk. Bear left along the river's south bank to a picnic area, small fishing dock, beach and wading area. You will climb upon some huge, smooth granite rocks here and there. The path continues to lovely cataracts where the Roaring Fork drops in elevation. At these falls, turn right to the ice caves, an old stage road and erratic boulders to complete the tour. For a longer, lovelier river walk, continue beyond the falls, first ascending some rocks, then edging the water. You will connect with the old stage road where the river trail ends. Bear right and return to your start via an enlarged loop not depicted on the sign.

Sidetrips may prove as pleasant as the designated route. Many footpaths, each with many branches, edge both banks of the river, upstream and down. Broad, flat rocks offer seating in a multitude of high view spots. Other trails terminate at water's edge. Just downstream from the parking area on the north bank is a log picnic table in the woods and a log bench on a tiny beach by the river.

Aspen to Destination: The Grottos is reached by driving 9.2 miles east on Route 82 from Mill and Main in Aspen. Exactly one mile beyond the Weller Campground sign make a sharp right onto a gravel road to the parking area. This entry is not marked and cannot be seen in advance. Toilet facilities are furnished, but no drinking water is available. A picnic table and a grill are adjacent to the parking area, but more private spots are found on a short stroll up or down either side of the river. Bring insect repellent as mosquitoes can be pesky here in a wet summer. To walk across the rocks, wear athletic shoes with nonslip soles. And carry drinking water on this and all excursions in the mountains.

The Roaring Fork Braille Trail

THE REMARKABLE BRAILLE TRAIL, FIRST OF ITS KIND ANYWHERE, MAKES A BRIEF educational outing for all members of the family. Twenty-two stations, marked by both Braille and printed plaques and connected by a guide wire, invite blind and sighted visitors to explore nature through senses other than the visual. The quarter-mile, gently undulating loop trail travels over rocky glacial moraine and soft evergreen needles, through fragrant forest and sun-warmed meadow, and alongside the symphonic river. This peaceful little spot offers an easy, hands-on way to learn about the natural world. Some visitors might choose to walk the trail blindfolded to sensitize themselves to sound, smell and touch.

Each station presents a simple message about the subalpine environment. At Station 10 the plaque reads: "The bark of the spruce tree on the left feels rough and scaly. A fir tree across the trail, on your right, has a smooth and pitted trunk."

Established in 1967 by biologist Bob Lewis and named to honor Louis Braille, who developed a tactile code for the blind, the Roaring Fork Braille Trail has inspired the development of over 60 such trails nationwide.

Aspen to Destination: Drive east on Route 82 for 12.4 miles from Mill and Main in Aspen. A sign reading "Braille Nature Trail 1000 feet" precedes a right turn to parking set amidst lodgepole pines. The trail lies east of Weller Lake and the Grottos and just west of Lost Man Campground and Reservoir. Elevation is 10,400 feet.

Weller Lake Hike

GENERAL AREA:	Midway
TRAILHEAD:	8.2 miles from Mill & Main in Aspen
	16.9 miles from rodeo in Snowmass Village
HIKING DISTANCE:	1.5 miles round trip
ELEVATION GAIN:	200 feet
LOW POINT:	9360 feet at trailhead
HIGH POINT:	9560 feet at Weller Lake
HIGHLIGHTS:	Tumbling cascades and water music
	Scar of a forest fire above lake
	Short sidetrips
	Alternate trailhead
FISHING:	Rainbow trout in Weller Lake
	Rainbow, brown, brook trout in RF River
	Mountain whitefish in RF River
NEARBY ATTRACTIONS:	The Grottos for a scenic stroll or picnic
	Braille Trail for a self-guided nature walk

Comments: The easy, wooded Weller Lake trail carries hikers to the Roaring Fork River, over footbridges, along a cascading stream, and to a sizable dark lake ringed by rocks and forest. The main route is safe for supervised small children. A sidetrip to river rapids, a climb above the lake, or a clamber over boulders at the water's edge is not recommended for the youngest hikers. Other trail spurs await curious visitors. This is a good early summer excursion; in a year of drought, the path's lovely waterfalls and streams may vanish before summer's end.

Aspen to Trailhead: Drive east 8.2 miles on Route 82 from Mill and Main in Aspen and look for a sign at left that reads "White River National Forest Campground - Weller." At right stands a small brown "Trailhead" sign with an arrow pointing right. There is space for about two cars just before this marker, and just beyond the sign lies an ample, off-road, gravel parking area in aspen trees. At the end of the lot is a Forest Service sign and a register box.

Trail Route: To the sign's right, a few steps descend to a dirt trail amidst aspens and lichen-clad boulders. Travel ahead on the wide main route to a fork and a wooden sign that directs you to the right toward an opening by the Roaring Fork River. (A short sidetrail at left also parallels the water.) Much cow parsnip—a huge, flat-topped white flower—blooms in this moist, sunny spot. Next, evergreens take over from aspens where the river is shallow and flows serenely over a flat bottom. The water glimmers gold-brown in sunlight. The trees are soft, friendly firs and prickly spruces. Passing under these conifers, you reach a path leading a few yards to the water's edge. This is a tranquil spot, without rapids or a swift current.

Continue on main trail where, by midsummer, bush honeysuckle displays shiny black twin berries embraced by leafy red bracts. There is purple vetch, a pea relative. And the abundant, green horsetail plant indicates wetness. Its stems are poisonous to grazing animals, and its texture is like that of a scouring pad.

Move alongside the quiet river, sometimes at water's edge. Cow parsnip here grows five feet tall, dwarfing young hikers. Approach a wooden bridge on the left, climb its five steps and cross the Roaring Fork. This is the route to the lake.

From the bridge you can see every colorful stone on the river's bottom and a gargantuan boulder downstream which marks the start of river rapids. A level sidetrail before the bridge-crossing leads to the rough water. There you will find rocks for sunning and a cool, pleasant place under spruces. But the rapids make it an unsafe place for impetuous children.

Exit the bridge, mount ten steps, and look for a sign pointing left for "Roaring Fork Overlook" and right for "Weller Lake Trail." (The left branch of the trail is a short spur to two bridges over tributaries feeding the Roaring Fork.)

Follow the Weller Lake sign toward the hike's destination. Cross a simple footbridge over a trickle that gurgles and bubbles as it emerges from beneath stones. The scent of the conifer forest is lovely, and the trees' needles are spongy underfoot. Some rocks and roots are embedded in the path that travels gradually uphill. A wooden sign on the right announces the "Collegiate Peaks Wilderness."

111

As it approaches a small boulderfield, the trail switchbacks left. When it next twists right, a waterfall is audible. About 20 feet off the route is a viewpoint for a beautiful tumble of white water. A tree trunk across this sidetrail indicates closure or wrong way. This is a standard indicator. Watch children carefully here.

Continue on the main path as it climbs in switchbacks. Ignore the many secondary trails. Melodic sounds precede a photogenic cascade plummeting through tall, straight evergreens. Turn left at a large rock and cross a substantial bridge over this racing water, outflow from Weller Lake.

After three gentle turns of the boulder-lined trail, Weller Lake fills the scene in front of you. A jumble of fallen trees distinguishes the lake's outlet, numerous rockfields ring the shoreline, and snow sits atop a broad ridge high above the lake. Upper slopes of Mount Shimer and New York Peak across the water exhibit the ravages of a 1980 forest fire.

There is no path around Weller Lake, but visitors can clamber over rocks to the water's edge where comfortable perches abound.

Hike Extension: An indistinct footpath climbs up to the left over rocks and deadfall to several viewpoints above the lake. It is steep and may be obstructed with prostrate trees and broken branches. But for careful, agile adults, the sidetrip may be a way to find solitude, serenity, and a cool breeze high above the dark water. Here you seem to be very far from civilization— an unexpected pleasure from a hike so short and so close to town. If you choose this sidetrip, descend to the lake with caution.

Alternate Trailhead: A pleasant, overgrown little trail connects Route 82 to the bridge crossing the Roaring Fork. It begins at the small parking area where a "Trailhead" sign is posted. This is just short of the main Weller Lake parking lot and is directly opposite the "Weller Campground" sign. The narrow path twines through shrubs and tall grasses to a rock overlooking a pretty beaver pond. Sedges grow in the shallows and an old beaver lodge confirms the pond's origins. Walk to the right, following the path which dips into muddy spots and rises onto dry areas as it parallels Route 82, sometimes visible through the aspen trees. Descend slightly, push through

Weller Lake Forest Fire

Above the expanse of Weller Lake on the flanks of Mount Shimer and New York Peak, tree skeletons stand where once flourished a green forest of subalpine fir and Engelmann spruce. On July 17, 1980 an abandoned campfire ignited the timber, burning approximately 900 acres. A containment strategy was used with control lines constructed only below the fire. On the steep upper slopes of the mountains, the flames were allowed to burn into snowfields and rocky outcroppings, where they were extinguished naturally.

Flowering plants and quaking aspens have colonized the open space, creating a nursery environment for the infant evergreens that will again dominate—in 300 to 400 years. This is a typical example of ecological succession: The fresh aspens that will shelter the slow-growing conifers will someday perish from the shade of the larger trees. Fire is a natural part of that process of regeneration: a forest cleansing and soil enrichment mechanism that permits the growth of new life that, in turn, nourishes other plants, birds and mammals.

some willows, and emerge at the footbridge on the main trail. If you choose to return by this alternate route, cross the bridge and bear slightly left into the willows to find the way back to the road.

Wilderness: Collegiate Peaks   USGS map: New York Peak

Midway Pond Hike

GENERAL AREA:	Midway
TRAILHEAD:	13.9 miles from Mill & Main in Aspen
	22.5 miles from rodeo in Snowmass Village
HIKING DISTANCE:	4.8 miles round trip
ELEVATION GAIN:	1500 feet
LOW POINT:	10,500 feet at trailhead
HIGH POINT:	12,000 feet at Midway Pond
HIGHLIGHTS:	Spacious alpine plateau, flowers, rivulets
	Picturesque pond with scenic backdrop
	Elk Mountains and Continental Divide
	Optional hike extensions to peak or pass
FISHING:	None on trail. See Lost Man Reservoir.
NEARBY ATTRACTIONS:	Lost Man Reservoir for rainbow trout
	The Grottos for a scenic stroll or picnic
	Braille Trail for a self-guided nature walk
	Ghost town of Independence for local history

Comments: Midway is one of the more challenging hikes described in this guide. The trail switchbacks relentlessly through lodgepole pines to gain about 1000 feet of altitude in the first mile. The final 500 feet of ascent carries hikers gently upward through spruce-fir forest, willow thickets and alpine meadows. While the lower trail may be hot and dry, the tundra above may be cool and wet with snowmelt. Carry a warm layer and dry socks, and schedule this hike for morning hours when weather is more stable. Ambitious hikers may climb a nearby peak to 13,033 feet—one of five thirteeners in the Williams Mountains—or descend 160 feet to Midway Pass about a mile beyond the pond.

Aspen to Trailhead: Drive east on Route 82 for 13.9 miles from Mill and Main in Aspen, passing Weller Campground, The Grottos, Lincoln Creek Gulch turnoff and the Braille Trail en route. Park on the left side of the road opposite Lost Man Campground in the Lost Man Reservoir parking area.

114

Trail Route: Adjacent to the parking lot stand several Forest Service placards. On a post are brown signs for "Midway Trail No. 1993" and "Lost Man Trail No. 1996" to the left and "Lost Man Reservoir" to the right.

Follow the path as it heads west, to the left, through trees and over a footbridge. This moist area is home to willows and wildflowers, including bog gentian, monkshood, cinquefoil, harebell and paintbrush. After about a quarter-mile, the trail forks at a sign and the first of many switchbacks. Bear slightly left and uphill for the Midway Trail; the path to the right leads to nearby Lost Man Reservoir, to Lost Man Trail and, eventually, to South Fork Pass.

The Midway Trail is easy to follow as it twists uphill through lodgepole pines. The trees do not obstruct views of the reservoir below, Lost Man Creek Valley beyond to the north, and the peaks of the Continental Divide to the south and east. Though the trail here is monotonous with its repeating hairpin turns and steady grade, the carpet of needles underfoot softens the surface. Rocks are few. This is the most taxing part of the trip, but frequent pauses for scenery-appreciation and for rehydration make it quite tolerable. When the switchbacks end after a mile, you have climbed 1000 feet, two-thirds of the hike's elevation gain.

At the final sharp turn, bear left at a rock wall and boulder field. Note a small black and white National Forest Wilderness sign tacked to a tree trunk. The lodgepoles are replaced by Englemann spruces and subalpine firs, companions in the high-altitude subalpine life zone.

As the trail meanders toward treeline, you reach a wonderful viewspot where, to the west, the striking white face of Snowmass Mountain is unmistakable. Left of the white mountain rise the two Maroon Bells and broad Pyramid Peak. All measure over fourteen-thousand feet. The view south includes 13,988 foot Grizzly Peak, a square-topped mountain with vertical ridges lined with snow. Far to its left is broad, snow-spotted La Plata Peak, fifth highest "fourteener" in Colorado.

115

Continue on the lightly wooded path where, under the trees, bloom Jacob's ladder, parrotsbeak lousewort and various hues of paintbrush. About two miles from the trailhead, rolling alpine spaces spread out before you. Walk over boggy meadowland, step across innumerable, dulcet rivulets of snowmelt, and brush past shrubby willows. The dampness and sunshine nurture an exuberant garden of alpine flowers, beginning with a carpet of white marsh marigolds in June and culminating in a show of elegant gentians in August. The trail meanders northwest through this beautiful, expansive terrain. Early in the summer the route might be snowy or faint, but it would be difficult to become disoriented here. The Williams Mountains are the wall to the northeast, right of the route, while directly west rise the distinctive peaks of the Elk Range. Occasionally, the Independence Pass road is visible in the valley below.

Savor here the loveliness of the tundra landscape—a vast panorama of undulating land dotted with tarns, watered by tinkling trickles from snowbanks, ornamented by tiny, colorful blossoms underfoot. It is a place both serene and overwhelming.

On their western expedition in 1804-06, explorers Lewis and Clark found that Native Americans from the Great Plains ventured into the mountains to cut certain tall, straight pines for their teepee poles. The tree has since been known as the **Lodgepole Pine**. Stout, twisted needles cluster in pairs; stalkless, small cones are tucked inside the tree; and the orange-brown bark is thin with small, loose scales. The asymmetrical cones open only when heated by fire, thus replanting the burned forest. Look for lodgepoles on the lower Midway Trail, the Braille Trail and along the road to Grizzly Reservoir.

A half-mile after departing the woods, the trail approaches a knoll festooned with small evergreens. Behind this hillock lies Midway Pond, picturesque and inviting. Tucked in a verdant hollow below the path, this spot suggests rest, meditation or a picnic. A huge rock overlooking the water seems sculpted for seating. In the distance stands pointed Castle Peak, a "fourteener," and Conundrum Peak, its attached mate. To the right of this dominant mass is Cathedral Peak with its multiple ascending spires.

Hike Extensions: For ambitious hikers, there are opportunities for exploration. The trail continues across this high plateau and descends 160 feet to Midway Pass about a mile from the pond. It is rare for a pass to lie below a hike's high point. To the northeast, an unnamed peak of the Williams Mountains rises to 13,033 feet. There is no trail, but a cross-country scramble up its grassy slope rewards with sight of the Williams Mountains' other peaks and with an expanded panorama of the exquisite Elk Range. Elevation gain from pond to peak is 1000 feet. Scrutinize the sky for storm clouds before attempting the ascent.

Wilderness: Hunter Fryingpan

USGS maps: Mt. Champion, Thimble Rock, Independence Pass

Golden-Mantled Ground Squirrel
A Silent Socialite

THEY SEEM TO BE EVERYWHERE—QUIETLY TUNNELING under steps to Snowmass Village condominiums, begging for handouts at Crater Lake, socializing with hikers atop Buckskin Pass, pirating goodies from unwary campers. Often mistaken for an overgrown chipmunk, this pert, genial, burrowing rodent is a distinctly separate member of the squirrel family.

Unlike the widespread, tiny chipmunk, the larger Golden-mantled Ground Squirrel lives only in North America's high western mountains from 7000 feet of altitude to treeless tundra. *Spermophilus lateralis* is plentiful here and easy to identify. Each of his sides is marked by one white stripe bordered by black stripes—lines ending at his shoulders, not his nose. This lack of facial streaks is characteristic of all ground squirrels. Between his stripes, the squirrel's back is gray-brown, and his belly white. He is sometimes called "copperhead" for the russet or golden color of his face, neck and shoulders—the "golden mantle" of his common name. His furred tail is of moderate size but not bushy, and his total length may be 8.5 to 13 inches. His shiny black eyes are rimmed with white, and his cheek pouches help him gather food.

Ground squirrels excavate a tunnel maze up to 100 feet in length with entrances under logs, tree roots, shrubs or rocks. They cache food for wakeful moments during a long winter hibernation and for the first meals of springtime. By then, the heavy fat accumulated during summer feasting is largely gone. The squirrel is omnivorous, eating seeds, nuts, fruits, herbs, fungi, eggs, insects and carrion. Despite their comic or

118

brazen solicitations of humans, ground squirrels remain healthier when dining on their natural foods.

An average of five young are born in the spring or early summer and will produce their own families the next year. Weasels, hawks, coyotes and winter starvation are the ground squirrels' enemies. Chattering Uinta chipmunks are often neighbors of the silent copperhead.

"I think I could turn and live with animals, they are so placid and self-contain'd, I stand and look at them long and long."

—WALT WHITMAN

Lost Man Reservoir

ADJACENT TO THE INDEPENDENCE PASS ROAD, LOST MAN RESERVOIR AND environs offer multiple pleasures for families interested in fishing and outdoor exploration. The reservoir is 13.9 miles east on Route 82 from Mill and Main in Aspen. Parking is left of the highway across from Lost Man Campground. A short walk through trees and over a bridge leads to the water. Elevation here is 10,600 feet.

The reservoir is stocked periodically with 4600 ten-inch rainbow trout over the summer months. Spilling into the reservoir's north end is Lost Man Creek, unstocked but supporting brook trout. A level trail edges the creek, offering easy hiking for anyone wishing to survey this pretty valley. The route crosses a few tributaries as it moves in and out of trees and through wildflower meadows. The trail heads north, eventually climbing to South Fork Pass, and loops east and south to Lost Man and Independence Lakes. The shorter Midway Trail also begins near the reservoir and switchbacks uphill to an alpine meadow and pond.

> **Lost Man Creek** was named by early prospectors for Billy Koch, a fellow who lost his way by following the wrong drainage en route to Leadville from Aspen. A question remains: Did he ever return?

INDEPENDENCE PASS

The Ghost Town of Independence
Tundra
Linkins Lake Hike
Independence Lake Hike
Yellow-Bellied Marmot
Elephanthead

INDEPENDENCE PASS REGION

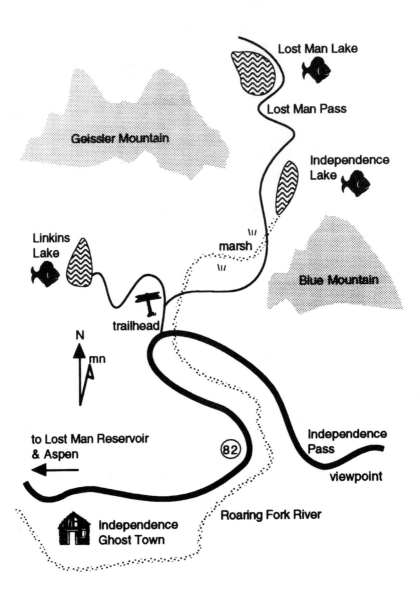

The Ghost Town of Independence

O
N JULY 4, 1879 BILLY BELDEN AND HIS PARTNER STRUCK GOLD NEAR
the Roaring Fork Camp, a tiny mining bivouac high in a mountain
valley just west of the Continental Divide. The Leadville prospector called his claim "Independence" in honor of the national celebration.
This remote area's geologic and geographic features had been mapped by
the Hayden Survey in 1873 and 1874. Prospectors were eager to check
out promising reports. They could do so after the land was ceded by the Ute
Indians in an 1878 treaty. Belden's discovery in a place the Utes had called
Hunter Pass was to transform a hunting ground into a mining town. A tent
community sprouted almost immediately and took its new name from the
first claim.

By 1880 the camp housed 300 people in crude log cabins. The Farwell
Mining Company, established a year earlier, acquired ownership of major
mines in the area and built both a stamp mill for crushing ore and a large
sawmill for mine construction. The stamp mill began operations in 1881
and produced $100,000 worth of gold that first year. A primitive stage road
was completed, linking Independence to Aspen and Leadville, and the
camp grew to 500 people, who supported four grocery stores, four boarding
houses, three saloons and a newspaper.

The Town of Independence was home to rugged types. Built in a mountain
meadow at 10,880 feet, it was snow-covered from early October through
May. Only the hardy could endure the work and the weather. But at least
1500 people resided there by 1882. Three post offices served the
community, and the 40 businesses included a bank, several hotels, and
many gambling halls, saloons and brothels. Independence was renamed at
least five times, a practice common to mining settlements.

But 1882 was to be the mining town's last boom year. Gold production plummeted; the mill operated only sporadically; miners and businesses moved to Aspen. In 1887, when two railroads raced to lay tracks linking Aspen to the outside world, lonely Independence was doomed. By 1888 the camp had fewer than 100 people, and by 1900, it was no more than a ghost town. Scattered buildings stand today.

A summer caretaker is available to answer questions and leads free guided tours daily except Mondays. Brochures, privies and a picnic table are on site.

At the western edge of Independence, an old road, now a foot trail, climbs the southern wall of the valley, passing many abandoned mines and cabins on its way to Green Mountain. The Roaring Fork River, however, lies between Route 82 and the trail. A ford of the river should not be attempted in early summer.

Aspen to Destination: Scenic Route 82 bisects the old townsite about four miles short of Independence Pass. Drive 16 miles east on 82 from Mill and Main in Aspen and look for roadside parking on the right. Ruins lie both above and below the road and dot hillsides throughout the area.

Tundra

A visit TO INDEPENDENCE PASS OR A HIKE TO LINKINS OR INDEPENDENCE Lake is a superb introduction to the land above the trees. For there is a life zone with an uncommon ecology, a harsh environment demanding specialized adaptations, a place imprisoned by winter most of the year.

In the Russian language, tundra means "land of no trees." The Russian designation, possibly derived from similar Lapp and Finnish words, refers to barren plains and hills in the arctic, antarctic and mountainous regions of the world. Anywhere on Earth, tundra characteristics are the same: an undulating, spacious, treeless landscape; soil movement and patterns created by frost action; and a blanket of low vegetation. In central Colorado, the land of no trees begins at approximately 11,500 feet of elevation.

A drive from Aspen to Independence Pass carries visitors from a temperate climate to an arctic one. Here winter can exhibit its dominance even in July when snow and hail assault the flowers and bitter wind scours the peaks. Rain in town often means snow at the pass. Summer temperatures rarely rise above 60 degrees F and frost-free days average only 40 per year. The temperature drops about 30 degrees from foothills to alpine regions because the thin air of high elevation holds less heat. Lightning storms give added volatility to most summer afternoons. Average precipitation is 25 inches annually, with windswept areas receiving less moisture as the snow is blown away. There is twice as much ultraviolet radiation and 25 percent more light than at sea level. Intense sunlight, fierce winds, dry atmosphere and low soil moisture make tundra a high altitude desert.

This alpine land may appear barren at first glance, but it is, in fact, a world rich with life. Exotic plants—many minute and exquisite, a few oversize and ostentatious—hurry to bloom as snowbanks recede. The condensed growing season produces a dazzling botanical show. Tundra soil is thin, eroded by wind, water and glaciers. Most wildflowers, therefore, are deeply rooted perennials which may take years to mature. Stems and leaves are often waxy or hairy as protection against the environment. In the most exposed locations, plants form low cushions and mats but produce precious, miniature blossoms, often fragrant and glowing with color. It is on these weatherworn passes, ridgetops and steep slopes that spring arrives first. Where snow is blown into cirques and crevices, spring may not arrive at all.

Stunted and contorted, a few trees survive on tundra. Called krummholz, a German word meaning "elfin timber" or "crooked wood," these prostrate, twisted evergreens crouch in the lee of boulders where there is some protection from the merciless wind. These wizened survivors may be over a thousand years old. They have sprouted from seeds blown onto tundra from lower altitudes.

Abundant insect life exists as well, with flies important as pollinators of wildflowers. Few bees work here as they are restricted to temperatures over 50 degrees F. But even the hardier flies are immobilized when clouds pass across the sun. Though spiders scurry hither and thither among the rocks, snakes and lizards eschew this cold environment.

One bird only, the male white-tailed ptarmigan, never departs the tundra. This high-alpine grouse, pure white in winter and mottled brown in summer, has feathered feet and legs to protect against the cold. It nests on the ground, as do the few birds who breed here in summer: water pipits, horned larks, rosy finches and white-crowned sparrows.

The land above the trees is home all year to a generous assortment of small mammals: meadow voles, mice, shrews, ground squirrels, pocket gophers, pikas, weasels and marmots. They survive by storing food, by hibernating or by exhaustive hunting. Human visitors often encounter the tundra's small residents.

More surprising, perhaps, is the permanent presence of large, hoofed mammals in this rugged environment so devoid of shelter and abundant food. But shaggy white mountain goats roam precipitous cliffs; bighorn sheep forage for grasses and sedges in ridgeline meadows; and bull elk are seen wandering the high country in winter. Hikers who venture from popular routes are rewarded with sightings of these splendid animals.

Linkins Lake Hike

GENERAL AREA: Independence Pass
TRAILHEAD: 18.0 miles from Mill & Main in Aspen
26.5 miles from rodeo in Snowmass Village
HIKING DISTANCE: 1.3 miles round trip
ELEVATION GAIN: 493 feet
LOW POINT: 11,515 feet at trailhead
HIGH POINT: 12,008 feet at Linkins Lake
HIGHLIGHTS: Beautiful clear lake in a grassy bowl
Many tundra flowers
Expansive alpine views
Optional hike extension
FISHING: Rainbow trout in lake
NEARBY ATTRACTIONS: Ghost town of Independence for local history
Independence Pass for views, tundra, tarns
Lost Man Reservoir for rainbow trout

Comments: The Linkins Lake trail is steep but short. It is suitable for most young hikers and is an excellent introduction to high altitude hiking and to the fragile tundra landscape. The lake's perfect alpine setting and the panorama visible from the trail are justifications for energy expended. A cross-country tundra walk is an optional hike extension. Be prepared for cold conditions here and in other locales above treeline. And schedule this hike for morning hours as menacing weather is more likely in the afternoon. Some visitors may wish to try excursions at lower elevations before attempting this hike.

Aspen to Trailhead: Drive east on Route 82 for 18.0 miles from Mill and Main in Aspen. Here, at a hairpin turn about two miles beyond the ghost town of Independence and two miles short of Independence Pass, look for an open space to the road's left. Park here for trails to Linkins Lake, Independence Lake, and Lost Man Lake and Loop.

Trail Route: "Linkins Lake Trail No. 2183" begins at the parking area and ascends steeply above and to the left of the fledgling Roaring Fork River. The route guides hikers toward a glacial cirque, or rocky bowl, to the west. Wind through scratchy, shrubby willows as you climb on a well-trod dirt path. A few conifers are in evidence, but as the journey begins above treeline, timber is scarce. This is often a damp place, encouraging the growth of white marsh marigolds in July and red elephantheads in August.

 Soon the trail passes over water and leads to a brown sign pointing left for Linkins Lake Trail and right for Lost Man Trail. The narrow waterfall tumbling down the nearby hillside descends from Linkins Lake. It is an early contributor to the burgeoning Roaring Fork, which originates near Independence Lake.

Bear left and climb alongside the outflow from the lake above. A little cluster of Engelmann spruces decorates a small knoll. From the knoll bear right toward a round-top rocky butte. Wildflowers blooming here in midsummer include white American bistort bobbing on red stems, pale yellow bracted lousewort with fernlike foliage, dark purple Whipple's penstemon, and both rosy and orange paintbrushes.

Below to the right is a view of the Lost Man Trail to Independence Lake. It parallels the Roaring Fork, which is nourished by multiple snowmelt rivulets snaking down the steep sides of this valley. The green saddle in the distance ahead is a pass taking hikers over to Lost Man Lake from Independence Lake. The mountain to its right is Blue Mountain/Twining Peak. Left of the pass is Geissler Mountain.

The trail angles upward sharply. Continue to bear left where a trail branches right for a route over Geissler Mountain to South Fork Pass. This is a fine place to encounter marmots as they often forage nearby. To the west is the cirque that cradles Linkins Lake.

The track levels off just below the lip of the bowl. A high ridge wraps around this place, and a ribbon of snow rests atop it in July. A cairn, a rockpile route marker, sits left of the trail. Parry's primrose, glowing magenta, blossoms in the adjacent small tarn and in the creek created by the lake's outflow. The tarn, or small pond, may be present only in wet years. Geissler Mountain is directly north. And in the distance to the southeast rises LaPlata Peak, fifth highest mountain in Colorado.

Linkins Lake is undeniably pretty. The water has great clarity, and the far shore may be white with snow in summer. The lake's periphery is level and grassy—a hospitable place for peaceful contemplation or a picnic. The wraparound ridge is enclosing, attractive. Trout break the water's surface. High on the hillside across the lake, a cabin and a mine are secreted just below and to the left of a rocky outcropping.

Wildflower sleuths may discover special alpine varieties underfoot at midsummer: tiny purple pygmy bitterroot/lewisia; rare red alpine lousewort; white bog/oregana saxifrage; and creamy-white alpine anemone.

Hike Extension: This locale offers good cross-country walking. Energetic visitors may wish to climb the grassy slope rising behind them as they face the lake. This sidetrip provides sterling views and a flat shelf of tundra sparkling with tarns and rivulets. Remember, however, that alpine tundra is delicate and slow to recover. To minimize impact on vegetation, step on rocks when possible and direct your group to spread out. Avoid walking single file.

Wilderness: Hunter Fryingpan

USGS map: Mt. Champion, Independence Pass

Independence Lake Hike

GENERAL AREA: Independence Pass
TRAILHEAD: 18.0 miles from Mill & Main in Aspen
26.5 miles from rodeo in Snowmass Village
HIKING DISTANCE: 3.5 miles round trip to Independence Lake
4.1 miles round trip to Lost Man Pass
5.3 miles round trip to Lost Man Lake
ELEVATION GAIN: 975 feet to Independence Lake
1285 feet to Lost Man Pass
350 foot loss from pass to Lost Man Lake
LOW POINT: 11,515 feet at trailhead
HIGH POINT: 12,490 feet at Independence Lake
12,800 feet at Lost Man Pass
HIGHLIGHTS: A natural garden of tundra flowers
U-shaped, glacially carved valley above treeline
Two hike extensions from Independence Lake
FISHING: Brook trout in Independence Lake
Cutthroat and brook trout in Lost Man Lake
NEARBY ATTRACTIONS: Ghost town of Independence for local history
Independence Pass for views, tundra, tarns
Lost Man Reservoir for rainbow trout

Comments: This high altitude trek edges the Continental Divide as it moves north through a glacial valley made moist by the newborn Roaring Fork River, alpine swamps and a multitude of snowmelt tributaries feeding the river. It is a place of overpowering, austere beauty and fragile, transitory wildflowers. But its elevation makes it cold, as well as wet. Warm clothing and spare socks are recommended. Save this hike for a sunny morning after mid-July and retreat if a storm threatens. ·

Energetic members of a hiking party may choose to extend the alpine experience by climbing the extra 310 feet to Lost Man Pass, where views are expanded. A drop below the pass to Lost Man Lake should appeal to fishermen. Some visitors may wish to plan excursions at lower elevations before attempting this hike.

Aspen to Trailhead: Drive east on Route 82 for 18.0 miles from Mill and Main in Aspen. Here, at a hairpin turn about two miles beyond the ghost town of Independence and two miles short of Independence Pass, look for an open space to the road's left. Park here for trails to Linkins Lake, Independence Lake, and Lost Man Lake and Loop.

Trail Route: From the roadside parking area a distinct trail mounts left the infant Roaring Fork River, born in the valley traversed by the hike. A sign reading "Linkins Lake Trail No. 2183" stands next to a Forest Service registry box. A few minutes into the hike, step over water and approach a sign directing hikers left for Linkins Lake Trail and right for Lost Man Trail. Bear right toward a Hunter-Fryingpan Wilderness sign and parallel the water as you wind north through low, shrubby willows, past orange and rosy paintbrushes, and over small sidestreams. Elevation is gained gradually for the first half-mile and then becomes more apparent as you begin to climb toward the lip of a spacious, marshy basin.

The nearby horizon includes two dips, or passes. Directly ahead is Lost Man Pass above Independence Lake. To its left, northeast, is Geissler Pass, separating two summits of Geissler Mountain. The peak directly east on the Continental Divide at right is Blue Mountain, also named Twining Peak. Its elevation is 13,711 feet.

Just beyond the mile point, the path swings right to rise above the swampy basin and climbs again, mounting a slope in its approach to Independence Lake. Willows thin out with elevation gain, and grasses, sedges and flowers dominate. A backward look delivers sight of Linkins Lake, tucked above a glacial bench in a rocky cirque, or hollow, to the southwest. It perches about 500 feet above this hike's trailhead. Directly behind you, to the south, rises mighty Grizzly Peak at 13,988 feet. Its distant, dark face has vertical fissures packed with snow; it seems scarred by a giant claw.

As the trail levels off, it swings gently west, crossing outflow and edging the left shore of Independence Lake. It may disappear in boggy places. Look for cairns, rockpile markers, to guide you. The lake sits on the floor of a natural amphitheater. The break in the high surrounding wall ahead is Lost Man Pass. Water sounds, snow, mud and marsh marigolds are common here. Melting snowbanks nourish king's crown, queen's crown, and tiny, magenta fairy primroses, distinctive with their yellow eyes. Yellow Indian paintbrush is everywhere. Furry marmots reside near the lake and among the rocks at the pass and beyond. If you are patient and quiet, they may venture from their dens.

You are at 12,490 feet and perhaps feel the effects of high altitude. Rest and drink liquids.

Hike Extension: Hikers who feel acclimated to high altitude will enjoy the ascent to the pass where views include Lost Man Lake and the Hunter Fryingpan and Holy Cross wilderness areas. The steep path to Lost Man Lake descends the rough, crumbly wall of a glacial cirque, abandoned by ice more recently than the south side of the pass. Snow here may have a pinkish tinge. Called "watermelon snow," it is home to a green alga wearing a rosy-red gelatinous coat to protect it from ultraviolet radiation.

For a longer hike east of Independence Pass, see North Fork Lake Creek Trail in *The Aspen Dayhiker*.

Wilderness: Hunter Fryingpan

USGS map: Mt. Champion, Independence Pass

Yellow-Bellied Marmot
The Native Sybarite

THE MOST APPEALING SMALL MAMMAL IN THE ROCKIES RESEMBLES A floppy stuffed animal whose stuffing is a bit meager for his brown fur coat. Flumping along trails and roadsides near Independence Pass and the Maroon Bells is the ample, stocky Yellow-bellied Marmot. Largest member of the mountain squirrel family, *Marmota flaviventris* is also called Rockchuck, Woodchuck or Whistle Pig. He is identified by short legs, a black face with white markings, a golden belly, buff neck patches, small round ears, a blunt nose, and a bushy tail which flips upright when he runs. Adult weight is usually eight to 10 pounds and length varies from 18 to 30 inches.

Though found stationed on inhospitable high peaks and passes, the chunky marmot favors rocky regions near lush alpine meadows where he digs an elaborate burrow, feasts on green plants and sunbathes on boulders—a natural voluptuary. Only approaching danger and approaching winter energize this mellow mammal. Marmots are hunted by eagles, coyotes, bobcats and mountain lions. A sharp whistle or chirp alerts other members of the colony, who duck into dens under rocks. Late summer triggers an active eating binge to build up fat reserves for the long hibernation to come.

Males are generous with their affections, and females bear three to six young in the spring. Yearlings are expected to move on to new territories and will live about 10 years.

Marmots often exhibit curiosity about humans, remaining on rocky lookouts to investigate hikers. Though the charm of this plump mountain resident may tempt you to toss tidbits of food, resist the urge. Marmots and all wild creatures remain heathier if their natural diets are not altered.

Elephanthead
Pink Elephants: The Real Thing

EVEN THE MOST FORGETFUL AMONG US CAN FOREVER RECALL THE NAME OF one wildflower. With an anatomy so like the head of an elephant, it almost trumpets its name. The plant's dense flower spike is a herd of little elephant faces, colored reddish purple to pink. Elephantheads colonize damp spots throughout the subalpine and alpine climate zones. Look for them in the Independence Pass region where they often share boggy spaces with the white marsh marigold.

An oddly shaped flower is responsible for this extraordinary look-alike. The upper petal is bulbous on top, creating the animal's forehead. It tapers into a long, graceful, upturned trunk. Three lower petals spread wide to form the red elephant's big ears and lower lip. Unbranched stems are red as well, and the narrow, green leaves are finely dissected, resembling those of a fern. Plant height varies from six to 20 inches.

Elephanthead is one of nine mountain louseworts, moisture-loving flowers with peculiar shapes and divided leaves. Superstitious farmers once believed that cattle who ate these flowers became infested with lice. Hence, lousewort, or *Pendicularis*. Elk graze, unharmed, on Elephantheads in early summer. The species name, *groenlandica*, indicates that the flower was discovered or originated in Greenland, but many botanists doubt its presence there. So while Elephanthead's botanical name is entirely misleading, its common name is absolutely perfect.

LINCOLN CREEK

The Ghost Town of Ruby
Anderson & Petroleum Lakes Hike
Northern Pocket Gopher
Grizzly Reservoir & Lincoln Creek

LINCOLN CREEK REGION

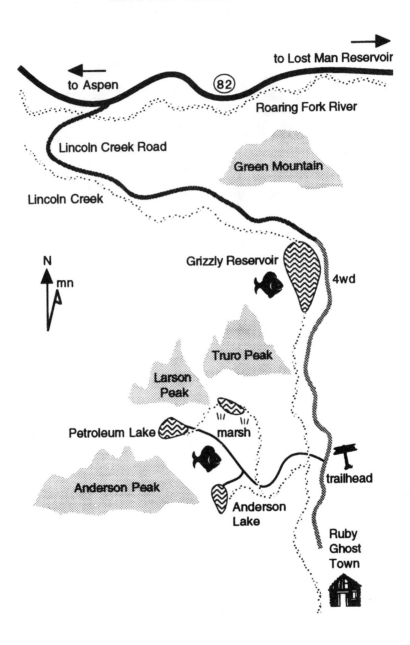

The Ghost Town of Ruby

RUBY HAD TO BE HOME TO THE MOST DELUDED OF OPTIMISTS. SITUATED IN a box canyon at 11,400 feet, the site seems to possess no favorable characteristics. The canyon's open end faces north, subjecting resident miners to the full impact of brutal storms. Towering mountains of the Continental Divide block the low sun in winter and limit its influence in spring and fall. Weather at 8000 feet is volatile; weather at treelimit can be downright frightening.

Located at the headwaters of Lincoln Creek, Ruby was at least 10 wilderness miles from the prospectors' path over Independence Pass. By today's roads, it lies 20 miles from Aspen and 60 miles from Leadville. Without a rail line or wagon road over the surrounding mountains to developed communities, the miners had no apparent means of transporting their ore to processing centers. That these rough men had dreams is certain; that they acknowledged reality is doubtful.

But with energy and hope they came, building cabins in this remote valley, constructing trails up the mountainsides and digging mines in the thin air at 12,400 feet. Visions of riches from the glittering minerals in the rocks must have overshadowed all discomfort.

Unemployed miners from Independence camp were the first to find veins of good ruby silver ore in the spring of 1880. "Ruby silver" is a rare, native, pure silver. Several settlements arose, the largest known as Hurst's Camp. Before the winter snows descended, the men had established the Lincoln Mining District and called the fledgling community South Independence. As was common in such places, the town's appellation was temporary. Was Ruby re-named for nearby Red Mountain or for the presence of ruby silver? Or did this change occur in 1900 when the Ruby Mines and Development Company began operations?

Though the Ruby digs produced well, the unrefined ore had to be hauled by burro packtrain over Red Mountain and through Taylor Park to a wagon road at Everett and then on to distant Leadville. The long journey, terrible roads and inefficient and costly transportation descimated profits. Many people gave up before the Ruby Mines Company supplied a concentrator and drilled a tunnel under Red Mountain. Another improvement was the 1906 construction of a better wagon road down Lincoln Creek Gulch to the Independence Pass road. Now that the ore could be shipped out from Aspen, Ruby limped on, attracting new miners.

But by 1912, hope dwindled as profits remained small. Ruby's remote location was forever its enemy. Today some deteriorating cabins, a stable and a boardinghouse mark the one-mile length of Ruby's old main street. A few replicas of original structures have been built on the privately owned site.

Aspen to Destination: To explore the Ruby townsite, drive 10.0 miles east from Aspen on Route 82 and turn right onto a rough dirt road at Lincoln Creek Gulch. A city car can maneuver the 6.5 miles to Grizzly Reservoir, *but a 4WD vehicle is needed* for the final miles to the old townsite. The ruins of scattered cabins mark the trailhead for the Anderson and Petroleum Lakes hike, 3.4 miles past the reservoir. More ghost buildings and the road's end are one mile ahead.

Anderson & Petroleum Lakes Hike

GENERAL AREA: Lincoln Creek Gulch

TRAILHEAD: 19.9 miles from Mill & Main in Aspen
28.6 miles from rodeo in Snowmass Village

HIKING DISTANCE: 2.0 miles round trip to Anderson Lake
4.0 miles round trip to Petroleum Lake

ELEVATION GAIN: 600 feet to Anderson Lake
1100 feet to Petroleum Lake

LOW POINT: 11,200 feet at trailhead

HIGH POINT: 11,800 feet at Anderson Lake
12,300 feet Petroleum Lake

HIGHLIGHTS: A memorable drive
Two accessible alpine lakes
Creeks, ponds, rivulets, wildflowers
Abandoned miners' cabins
Optional hike extension

FISHING: Rainbow trout in both lakes

NEARBY ATTRACTIONS: The Ruby townsite for local history
The Grottos for a sensational stroll
Braille Trail for a self-guided nature walk

Comments: The adventure begins as you negotiate the rough road to the trailhead. *A high-clearance 4WD vehicle is a necessity*, unless you want to add six miles to the hike. The landscape is wonderful, but the ride is bumpy. The hike, however, is fairly gentle as it meanders out of trees and onto spacious, rolling tundra. This is a superb high altitude locale with its plethora of flowers, lakes, ponds and mountain views. Old cabins remain from mining days at the Ruby camp. The one-mile hike to Anderson Lake can be extended with a trip to Petroleum Lake and with additional cross-country exploration. A stream crossing might be awkward early in a wet year. Schedule this and all other alpine hikes for morning hours. Carry a warm clothing layer and coverings for head and hands. Some visitors may wish to plan excursions at lower elevations before attempting this hike.

Aspen to Trailhead: Drive east on Route 82 toward Independence Pass. At 10.0 miles from Mill and Main in Aspen turn right onto a rough dirt road entering Lincoln Creek Gulch. Proceed downhill for 0.5 miles and pass the entrance to Lincoln Creek Campground, staying left at the fork. Move alongside the creek past camping sites and trailheads, through woods and open spaces. Near Grizzly Reservoir at 6.5 miles from Route 82, look for the Portal Campground sign near Grizzly Lake trailhead. Here begins the truly rugged section of the road.

Bump along beside a grassy meadow, occasionally splashing through water. Tall evergreens are scattered about, and low willows bunch in damp places. Lincoln Creek bisects the valley. Signs read "Road closed" and "Road damage"—reminders to drive with caution. Ahead rises a distinctive, jagged mountain, Anderson Peak. Truro Peak, rising to 13,282 feet, is across the valley on the right.

The sunny meadow is home to lovely wildflowers. In late July puffy white American bistort bobs on red stems, shrubby cinquefoil is dotted with bright yellow flowers, and rosy avens/pink plumes stand with drooping heads. Pass a boulderfield on the left. Blue sky pilots bloom by the road and in the rocks. It seems a good place for pikas. A lacy waterfall tumbles down the cliff face at right. As you proceed, look for a cabin on the left and a rocky gorge opposite.

At 9.9 miles from Route 82, turn right from this main road and ford Lincoln Creek. A roofless log cabin is visible across the creek and marks the ford. Another crumbling dwelling sits below the first. Park near this spot.

To reach more ruins of the Ruby mining camp, continue for about a mile to the end of Lincoln Creek Road. The snowy guardians of this basin are peaks on the Continental Divide.

Trail Route: Begin by walking up a rocky 4WD road left of the roofless cabin. Remains of Ruby's buildings are visible to the south. Anderson Creek creates a little waterfall as it tumbles toward Lincoln Creek. The road turns toward a green metal gate. Signs here ban parking and all-terrain vehicles. Additional wooden signs announce "National Forest Wilderness" and "Petroleum Trail No. 1991."

Beyond the gate is a tidy log cabin with an outhouse in back. A tiny solar collector perches on the roof, and huge logs are piled ready for splitting. Private property, such as this, exists in small pockets within national forest boundaries.

The old road, now used only as a foot trail, continues gradually uphill through spruces and alongside the noisy creek to a second gate. Hikers can pass easily around both barriers. Much timber lies nearby, perhaps felled when the road was cut long ago. Walk toward ragged Anderson Peak with its vertical, snow-filled crevices. The mountain is part of a high ridge enclosing both lakes. In midsummer, rosy paintbrush has started to bloom, white brookcress flowers near puddles, and much yellow bracted lousewort borders the trail.

Two cabins were built near the path. The one at left is a jumble of logs. The cabin on the right is collapsing, but once it was snug and dry with glass windows and a metal roof. Within, two bed frames stand side by side. Adjacent to this ruin is a vigorous sidestream augmenting Anderson Creek. Scout for a narrow place or for a spot with exposed stepping stones. Walk over a small rise to another water crossing, easier than the first.

Tall trees vanish as you ascend from the subalpine zone to tundra, but several colors of paintbrush brighten the austere landscape. The trail forks as you approach Anderson Lake. Bear left across a flat, damp area into a basin that contains the lake. Anderson Creek burbles alongside the

> Anderson Lake's milky blue color is due to **glacial rock flour** suspended in the water. The flour, or powder, which gives alpine lakes a pale turquoise hue, is produced by the slow, grinding movement of rock and ice masses. The water in Petroleum Lake is a deep green, colored by micro-organisms, and without glacial flour.

trail. Sawtoothed Anderson Peak, standing 13,631 feet, is the lake's imposing backdrop. Its three prominent points connect to an undulating ridge with three humps. Larson Peak, with a similar craggy appearance, is behind you to your right. A summer snowpack may linger at the lake's far end. A small island is host to a few evergreens. Many stones edge the water, and some grasses and sedges soften the earth. The major characteristics of a tundra landscape are exhibited at this elevation of 11,800 feet.

To reach Petroleum Lake, one mile to the northwest, backtrack to the nearby trail junction. Follow the right-hand path, which loops around a rough, bare, butte-like peak to approach the higher lake. The grade is gentle here. A small sidestream cuts the trail on its journey to a creek below on the right. Stunted Englemann spruces cling to a knoll at left. To the far right, old mining roads mar a red slope. The ground is soggy underfoot. Purple pygmy bitterroot and yellow western paintbrush bloom at midsummer.

The path winds left around the butte to pass between it and Larson Peak, apricot in color, rough and crumbly. The taller of its two summits measures 12,908 feet. As the trail bends left, it becomes a single track. A large pond is visible to the right in a boggy lowland area ablaze with wildflowers: yellow alpine avens, white marsh marigold, magenta Parry's primrose and creamy alpine anemone. Blue chimingbells are everywhere in August. This spot is rich with bright colors and the melodic sounds of moving water. A big hole near the trail suggests an old miner's dig.

As you begin the steep final climb to Petroleum Lake, you can spot a small pond linked to the larger one by a rivulet. Snowfields may persist here in July and may be pink in color—a natural phenomenon known as "watermelon snow." A cascade drops left of the trail from the ridgetop above. Petroleum Lake is hidden there, and the waterfall is outflow from the lake. For a direct approach, be certain to ascend the hill just

Watermelon Snow

Hikers may be puzzled by patches of pink snow encountered on high country summer journeys. These alpine snowbeds nourish more than the glacier lilies and snow buttercups growing at their peripheries. They are home to a minuscule green alga encased in a rosy gelatinous coat. The red pigmentation of this microorganism begins to tint snow in May and June when melting provides water needed for growth. The coating is thought to protect the alga from radiation damage. These red cells, which concentrate airborne radiation, may be detected without a hand lens.

While watermelon snow has a certain eye appeal, do not eat it or melt it for drinking water—unless you are seeking a natural laxative.

right of the falling water. (The lower, faint 4WD road makes a loop to reach the lake from the north.)

This sharp incline moderates as you advance. At ridgeline, you can see Petroleum Lake ahead, beyond a stretch of grass. The barren rock wall above the water is snow-speckled, a dark brownish-gray. A butte anchors the lake's west end. Behind you to the north is Larson Peak and a rocky outcropping ornamented by a few stunted trees. It is a beautiful setting, a wonderful alpine panorama and an ideal place for a pause or picnic when the sun is warm. But the wind is often powerful here, and temperatures can be frosty on an overcast day.

Hike Extension: To lengthen the hike by cross-country walking, climb the ridge to the right of the lake. Continue over rolling tundra where smaller lakes, ponds and tarns are tucked in hollows here and there. It is possible to explore for a long while across softly undulating turf and over and around knolls. Many delightful surprises await the adventurer in this lovely land above the trees.

Wilderness: Collegiate Peaks

USGS maps: Independence Pass, New York Peak

Northern Pocket Gopher

Alpine Ghost Gardener

RARELY GLIMPSED BUT CONSPICUOUS BY HIS LABORS, THE ENERGETIC NORTHern Pocket Gopher is widespread throughout the Colorado mountains. Large, fan-shaped mounds of earth mark the entrances to his burrow—a tunnel system that may be 500 feet in length and represent nearly three tons of excavated soil. He can dig a tunnel more than 100 feet long in a single night. *Thomomys talpoides* lives nearly all of his life underground and is the only exclusively burrowing animal on the alpine tundra.

While a dirt mound always characterizes a gopher's territory, a unique sign is evident in the weeks after snow has vanished. Mountain terrain is crisscrossed by three-dimensional road maps—called gopher cores, garlands or eskers. These long, sinuous coils of earth, about two inches high, reveal the gopher's winter travels. He forages beneath the snow for vegetation and then plugs his snow tunnels with soil from subterranean excavations. To summer hikers, gopher cores are familiar features of the mountain landscape.

Pocket gophers profoundly influence alpine vegetation patterns as they bring subsoil to the surface, distribute seeds, bury plants that decompose, aerate the soil, recycle minerals, and add their own excreta and their organic remains when they die. By turning over the earth, these elusive rodents encourage a colorful, flowery community known as a "gopher garden."

West of the Continental Divide, the sturdy Northern Pocket Gopher is colored a rich brown. His eyes and round ears are small, of little use in a dark underworld. But highly sensitive whiskers help the gopher feel his way along a tunnel; and tactile nerve endings in his hairless tail allow him to gather information when in reverse. Powerful forelimbs have impressive claws, and yellowish-orange incisors are exposed in front of his lips. Fur-lined cheek pouches are external and used for carrying food. Total length is 6.5 to 9.5 inches and weight is less than five ounces. While up to 20 gophers may share an acre of lush meadow, their burrows do not intersect, and, except when mating, gophers are decidedly hostile to their neighbors.

Nest chambers are sometimes dug high in the snowpack as tunnels below fill with spring meltwater. Young gophers are sexually mature and independent after a few months in the maternal nest.

Grizzly Reservoir and Lincoln Creek

A POPULAR PLACE FOR FAMILY FISHING TRIPS, LINCOLN CREEK GULCH OFFERS both a roadside creek and Grizzly Reservoir as destinations. Over a period of several summer months, 2000 ten-inch rainbow trout are stocked in Lincoln Creek and 10,000 ten-inch rainbows are planted in the reservoir. A 10-mile drive east on Route 82 from Mill and Main in Aspen brings you to the gulch entrance. The road is narrow and rocky, and a 4WD vehicle is ideal transportation; but the route can be negotiated in a city car, preferably old, as far as the reservoir, 6.5 miles from Route 82. Drive slowly and with caution. The early portion is rough and winding; the latter section has fewer bumps and curves. Elevation at the reservoir is 10,560 feet.

Beyond Grizzly Reservoir, where the road is 4WD only, are both the trail to Anderson and Petroleum Lakes and the Ruby townsite. Consult **The Aspen Dayhiker** for treks to both Grizzly Lake and Tabor Lake, also accessed from Lincoln Creek Gulch.

"The gods do not deduct from man's allotted span the hours spent in fishing."

—BABYLONIAN PROVERB

146

DOWNVALLEY

DOWNVALLEY REGION

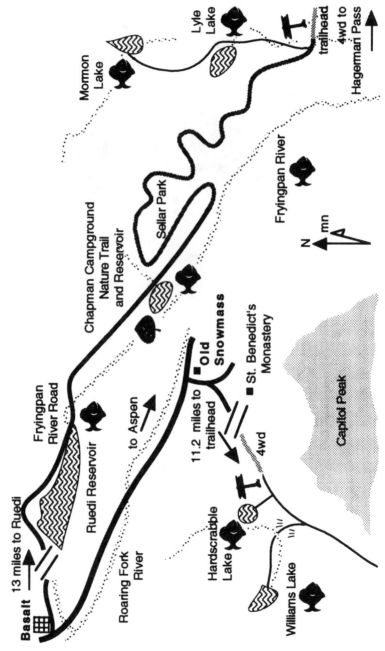

Basalt

13 miles to Ruedi

Fryingpan River Road

Ruedi Reservoir

Roaring Fork River

to Aspen

Chapman Campground Nature Trail and Reservoir

Sellar Park

Mormon Lake

Lyle Lake

trailhead

4wd to Hagerman Pass

Fryingpan River

N   mn

Old Snowmass

11.2 miles to trailhead

4wd

St. Benedict's Monastery

Hardscrabble Lake

Williams Lake

Capitol Peak

Basalt and Beyond

A CENTURY AGO THE FEW HAMLETS DOWNVALLEY FROM ASPEN OWED THEIR existence to a modern marvel, the railroad. While some tiny rail stops all but vanished when train service ended in the 20th century, others evolved into entities as different from each other as they are from their origins. The Emma post office and store are historical footnotes, but the old Basalt train depot functions nicely as a bank in a Victorian town now booming as a recreational and residential hub. The unpretentious ranching communities of old Snowmass and Woody Creek changed little after their separate railroad lines pulled out. Over the years many barns have been replaced by handsome houses, but each "downtown" is still confined to a single, rambling, multifunction building—each as distinctive as the people who gather there.

Downvalley squatters appeared around 1880 at the confluence of the Roaring Fork and Fryingpan Rivers. Two years later a tent village housed men working to produce charcoal for smelters in Leadville and Aspen. The brick, beehive-shaped kilns remain near downtown Basalt, a place known before 1895 as Frying Pan, Frying Pan Junction and Aspen Junction. The temporary character of Basalt changed in 1887 when the Colorado Midland Railroad brought passengers and freight to the Roaring Fork Valley. Although charcoal was being replaced by coke from coal mines at Spring Valley, Carbondale and Redstone, local men could now find railroad work in this new company town. Attracted to mountain land like that of northwest Italy and neighboring Switzerland, immigrants from the Italian region of Val d'Aosta arrived by train, settling down and welcoming their old neighbors and kin into the next century. Aosta surnames remain common in the Roaring Fork Valley.

A post office was established in 1890, and Basalt was incorporated in 1901. A 1912 town ordinance conveyed attitudes of the day: "... minors, Indians, idiots, women, and habitual drunkards are not allowed in the saloons." Basalt's position as a railroad town protected it from total ruin and obscurity after the silver debacle of 1893. But when the Colorado Midland halted operations in 1918, the town took a 30-year nap. Enthusiasm for outdoor recreation revitalized the entire region after World War II, and Basalt's splendid location lured fishermen and hunters. In 1994 the community counted 1800 residents, including many energetic entrepreneurs. Once regarded only as a bedroom community for chic Aspen, Basalt's old west charm and new west zest make it a distinct entity.

Basalt sits at an elevation of 6625 feet and is named for its geology. The dark, fine-grained, extrusive, igneous rock that caps nearby Basalt Mountain is a product of ancient lava flows.

Downvalley a few miles from Basalt is El Jebel, named for Henry Gillespie's large, elaborate country home and ranch. Gillespie, an Aspen founding father, moved to his retreat before silver was demonetized. Devastated by financial losses, he eventually sold the magnificent property, which was subdivided and successfully farmed. Crops of potatoes and hay sustained El Jebel during lean years after the Colorado Midland quit the valley. Modern El Jebel was born when mobile homes were trucked in to house workers on the Ruedi Dam project 30 years ago. The temporary dwellings became rooted. Now new homes sprout around them as many of today's workers commute to resort jobs in Aspen.

Carbondale was a commercial center before the railroad era. Fertile river-bottom land made farming viable; wildlife was abundant; the Roaring Fork and Crystal Rivers were rich with fish. William Dinkel became the area's first settler in 1881, dug the first irrigation ditches and operated a stagecoach station. By 1882, twenty families had homesteads, and soon Carbondale served as Aspen's pantry. As miners needed more provisions, the pioneers added sheep and cattle ranching to supplement crops and wild game. Potatoes became a mainstay of the agricultural economy for the next 50 years, and nearby coal deposits stimulated investment. When the railroads arrived in 1887, Carbondale's businesses thrived as coke from Redstone and marble from the Yule quarry were channeled through town.

Incorporated in 1888, Carbondale was named for the hometown of John Mankin and other Pennsylvania settlers. Today Carbondale's population rises monthly with transplants from California and Latin America, making it more than twice the size of Basalt. Agriculture now exists side by side with an expanding arts community.

The Ute Indians

EXACTLY WHEN THE NOMADIC UTE INDIANS ARRIVED IN COLORADO IS A MATTER for debate. Some scholars believe that the "Blue Sky People" arrived around 1400 A.D., while others note that the continuity of rock art styles argues for an extended prehistory. The Utes' precise origin is unknown, but a variation of their spoken language resembles that of the ancient Aztecs of Mexico. Fiercely independent, shy and isolationist, the Utes roamed the valleys and high country on foot, gathering plants and herbs and hunting deer, elk and bison. Their presence was first recorded by Spanish explorers in 1626. Seven bands of Utes were scattered from Colorado's Front Range well into Utah. Occupied territory included extreme southern Wyoming and northern New Mexico. Original hunting grounds extended beyond these perimeters.

In the mid-1600s the Utes acquired "magic dogs" from the Spanish, becoming the first western Indians to own horses in great numbers. They gained repute as excellent breeders and expert riders. Horse racing became the favorite sport of Ute men. These animals gave the Utes greater mobility, enlarged their territory and increased their contact with other tribes. Relations with the Spanish were strained, however, as the Indians frequently raided their outposts to steal horses. Retaliation resulted in death or enslavement of the natives. The Utes, in turn, defended their ponies from the Cheyenne and Arapaho.

In the Roaring Fork Valley, the Utes wintered in the lowlands along rivers, discovering the comfort and therapeutic value of the numerous hot springs around present-day Glenwood Springs. In summer, the native people moved into the high country—into their "Shining Mountains." These rugged ridges and peaks, now called the Elk Mountains, were to preserve their way of life until the 1870s, serving as an effective barrier to Plains Indians and white men alike. But while the Utes remained successful against other tribes, they could not repel the white man's obsessive pursuit of the gold, silver and coal that lay beneath their ancestral hunting grounds.

The few trappers visiting the Roaring Fork Valley as early as the 1820s were not a major threat to the Indians, who were respected for their fighting ability, their intelligent bartering, their superb horsemanship and their passionate protection of hunting grounds. But while these isolated Utes retained their independence for several decades more, Indians in other parts of the Colorado Territory were losing everything. Beginning in 1849, treaties, promises, deceptions, bribes and intimidation delivered land to the U.S. Government and hunger and homelessness to the Utes. And then the Pike's Peak Gold Rush of 1859 altered Colorado irrevocably as the whole nation eyed the region's potential mineral wealth.

The U.S. Government declared Chief Ouray, a Southern Ute, to be the premier chief and Ute negotiator. Ouray signed a treaty in 1868 assigning the southwestern Colorado Territory, essentially all of Colorado's western slope, to the Indians. White settlement was forbidden, and many miners were removed. The land began at the Continental Divide and included Aspen and the entire Roaring Fork Valley. Colorow, a chief of the unsophisticated White River clan, a splinter group of Northern Utes, opposed any treaty and rejected government authority. Just one year after Ouray's favorable agreement, the Ute Reservation Settlement Act expelled the White River Utes from the upper valley, later to be Aspen, and the region 10 miles west.

In 1873 Ouray and the Utes grudgingly granted a travel pass to Dr. F.V. Hayden and his U.S. Geological Survey team to map the western slope of the Rockies. Instructed to determine the economic potential of the region, botanists, geologists and topographers explored, assigning place names and recording evidence of gold, silver, coal and galena in the Roaring Fork and Crystal River Valleys. When the scientists were discovered poaching game on Ute land by Colorow and his White River band, they were reminded of treaty terms, their possessions were burned and they were chased from the Roaring Fork.

The remote valleys and peaks between Leadville, a mining mecca east of the Continental Divide, and the place that was to become Aspen was ceded to the whites in 1878, opening the land to prospectors who filed mining claims the next year. 1879 was, indeed, a disastrous year for the Utes. By then, all Ute holdings had been reduced from 16 million to 12 million acres, and the Ute population, 8000 in 1859, was down to 4000. The White River Utes hung on, resentful of the dictates of Nathan Meeker, director of the White River Indian Agency in northwestern Colorado. Meeker insisted that the Indians give up their migratory hunting expeditions, that they attend church services and that they plow the land as farmers—an act the Utes considered both degrading and a desecration of the earth. Believing the Indians to be lazy, Meeker denied them government-allocated food, plowed their race track and threatened to kill their beloved ponies. In the revolt that followed, Meeker and other white Agency employees were killed and mutilated, and their women and children kidnapped. Old Chief Quinkent was held responsible and jailed without charge at Fort Leavenworth, but some suspected that Colorow initiated the murders.

That tragedy sealed the fate of all Utes. The Southern tribes were banished to reservations in extreme southern Colorado. Colorow and his renegade White River band were driven onto a Utah reservation, leaving behind lush mountain valleys and abundant game for barren land that Brigham Young had declared unfit for human habitation. By 1920 only 2000 Utes survived on reservations in Utah and southern Colorado.

Ute Chief Colorow

THE ROARING FORK VALLEY, NOW POPULAR WITH HIKERS, CLIMBERS, cyclists, fishermen and skiers, was once a hunting ground of the flamboyant Ute Chief Colorow. Born to a Comanche father and Jicarilla Apache mother, Colorow was kidnapped as a child and raised with the Moache Ute clan. After Colorow left the Moache to join the White River band, an isolationist branch of the Northern Utes, he became an acknowledged chief. Leadership, not lineage, was paramount to the Utes.

Colorow, as were most Native Americans, was maligned by whites for his behavior and appearance. But he must have been memorable. Nearly six feet tall and sometimes weighing 300 pounds, the garrulous, intimidating chief was known to all settlers between Denver and Glenwood Springs. He frequently barged into pioneers' kitchens demanding food for himself and his entourage. He is said to have offered a string of ponies, highly valued by Utes, in trade for Clara Mandeville, a settler's wife. Disappointed in this effort, a disgusted Colorow derided the husband with "White man heap damn fool!"

Always resistant to white men's pressures, Colorow was reported to be the last Ute to forsake the Roaring Fork Valley for a Utah reservation. But notorious as a rebel and a wanderer, the colorful chief continued to steal into his old Colorado hunting grounds and frequented the warm, healing waters near Glenwood Springs. He was also legendary as a storyteller, and in his old age he related a moving tale of finding a white girl, lost and separated from her California-bound parents. Adopted by the Utes, Recha later married the young Colorow and journeyed with him until killed in a fall from her horse. The grieving husband buried her above the Yampa Springs and did not return for decades.

The Fryingpan River and Ruedi Reservoir

THE DOWNVALLEY TOWN OF BASALT SITS AT THE CONFLUENCE OF TWO RENOWNED Gold Medal Waters—the Roaring Fork and the Fryingpan. Veteran fisherman make faithful pilgrimages to this fortunate location while eager novitiates hope to de-mystify the subtleties of fly fishing. From little Basalt, a drive of thirteen miles beneath red cliffs and alongside the sparkling Fryingpan River brings visitors to vast Ruedi Reservoir, a place for additional fishing and for various water sports.

A bit more tranquil than the aptly named Roaring Fork, the Fryingpan is also more consistent in temperature and flow rate over the year because of the Ruedi Dam upstream. The river is highly regulated and produces fine trophy rainbow and brown trout—trout fattened by feasting on tiny freshwater shrimp hovering in quiet water near the dam. Between Basalt and Ruedi the river is stocked with 10,000 five-inch rainbow trout once a season. Browns are planted when populations drop. Upstream between the reservoir and Nast, the river is stocked with 3000 ten-inch rainbows over a period of several summer months. Brook trout sustain themselves both above and below the dam.

Use only artificial flies and lures in the Fryingpan, check on the location of catch-and-release sections, and know bag and size limitations.

Fishing guides often suggest easily accessible reservoirs and lakes to families with children. Ruedi has miles of shoreline and many fish cavorting below its glittering surface. The thousand-acre reservoir is generously planted annually with 15,000 five-inch splake (a marriage of brook and lake trout), 20,000 ten-inch rainbows and 100,000 two-inch kokanee salmon. Some

Fryingpan?

A name like "Fryingpan" just naturally provokes some questions. Without the elegance, strength or lineage of Crystal, Roaring Fork or Lincoln, it seems a curiosity. But nailing down the origin of Fryingpan is something like catching a trout with bare hands. Three tales reveal the breadth of local lore.

An oft-told version has Missouri trappers set upon by Indians who slew all but two. A wounded survivor was secreted in a cave by his companion who tied a frying pan to a pine tree's limb to mark the location. When the trapper returned with soldiers, he found his friend dead but the frying pan still fixed to the tree.

In a second story, two early gold prospectors lost much of their equipment while fording a river. Undeterred by this calamity, the pair used a salvaged frying pan to wash the river's sands in their pursuit of riches.

Another legend tells of prospectors about to camp on the upper part of a river when they noticed fresh signs of Indians. Fearing an encounter, they determined to retreat to Aspen by climbing over a mountain. But upon reaching the summit, they saw the Indians on the other side. One reportedly said, "We are just going from the frying pan into the fire," thereby naming both the valley and its river.

Mackinaw lake trout ply the waters but are not stocked. Elevation at the reservoir is 7766 feet.

Up the Fryingpan Road beyond Ruedi lies the Chapman Campground Nature Trail, a good addition to a family outing in this beautiful valley. Chapman Reservoir, another fishing venue, is adjacent to the campground.

Chapman Campground
Nature Trail and Reservoir

HAVE YOU EVER WONDERED ABOUT THE PORCUPINE'S DIET, THE VALUE OF dead trees or the peculiar placement of humongous boulders? Can you tell a lodgepole pine from a ponderosa? What is a serotinous cone? A skid trail? Witch's broom?

A visit to the Chapman Campground Nature Trail will answer these and other questions. A one-mile walk carries you through varied plant communities, known as ecosystems. A printed trail guide corresponds to stations marked by numbered posts. At station number 7, for example, the guide reads, "When Douglas-fir was first discovered, botanists were confused. Douglas-fir was not a Fir! Was it a Fir or was it a Hemlock? Actually it is its own species...."

The loop trail begins through lodgepole pines and aspens and winds gently uphill, moving away from the campground's lake, small Chapman Reservoir. Soon, gigantic, lichen-clad boulders are everywhere in the woods. Travel to vista sites, past logged, burned and reforested areas, and alongside wetlands. You will learn natural history and human history as you walk. The Chapman trail was dedicated in 1991 to the 100th Anniversary of the National Forest System.

Chapman Reservoir's dam was built by the Civilian Conservation Corps in the 1930s and is a miniature replica of the Hoover Dam on the Colorado River. The reservoir is stocked with 7400 ten-inch rainbow trout over a period of several summer months and makes a good family fishing destination.

Aspen to Destination: To visit the nature trail and reservoir, drive west for 18.1 miles on Route 82 from Mill and Main in Aspen. At the traffic signal for Basalt, turn right, cross a bridge over the Roaring Fork, turn left at a sign for the business district, pass over the Fryingpan and turn right onto Midland Avenue, which becomes Fryingpan River Road. Drive 28.6 miles from 82 and make a right turn at the sign for Chapman Campground. To fish, look for a left spur to the reservoir. To walk the nature trail, continue to the campground host's trailer where you bear left at a sign for Loop E. Drive a short distance and park near a gate. Right of the gate is a large Forest Service sign for the "Chapman Interpretive Trail." Brochures are in a box, and an arrow directs you to the left.

"Bragging may not bring happiness, but no man having caught a large fish goes home through an alley."

— ANONYMOUS

Lyle Lake Hike

GENERAL AREA: Downvalley/Fryingpan
TRAILHEAD: 61.1 miles from Mill & Main in Aspen
57.8 miles from rodeo in Snowmass Village
HIKING DISTANCE: 4.0 miles round trip
ELEVATION GAIN: 649 feet
LOW POINT: 10,720 feet at trailhead
HIGH POINT: 11,369 feet at Lyle Lake
HIGHLIGHTS: Large lake in a spacious alpine setting
Gorgeous hike extension to Mormon Lake
Outstanding scenery en route to trailhead
FISHING: Brook and lake trout in Lyle Lake
Brook trout in Mormon Lake
NEARBY ATTRACTIONS: Small town of Basalt on Fryingpan River
Chapman Campground Nature Trail
Ruedi and Chapman Reservoirs

Comments: This is the perfect trip for those who like a long, scenic drive paired with a short, scenic hike. The route winds along the Fryingpan River, below towering red pinnacles, above the huge Ruedi Reservoir and into the mountains of the Sawatch Range. *A 4WD vehicle is good security on the latter section of road.* Lyle Lake is a pleasant walk alongside a lively creek and through pastoral meadows. The recommended hike extension to Mormon Lake delights with dramatic sights of peaks and ponds at every twist of the trail.

Aspen to Trailhead: Drive west on Route 82, passing intersections for Snowmass Village and old Snowmass. At 18.1 miles from Mill and Main in Aspen, turn right onto Basalt Avenue at the traffic signal for Basalt. Set your odometer here. Cross a bridge over the Roaring Fork River, bear left at a gas station and a sign for "Downtown Business District," cross the Fryingpan River and turn right onto Midland Avenue, Basalt's main street. Midland is 0.3 miles from Route 82.

Follow Midland, which quickly becomes Fryingpan River Road, up a beautiful river valley to Ruedi Reservoir. Wind above the reservoir and continue past tiny Meredith and Thomasville and the dirt roads to Eagle and Burnt Mountain. At 28.6 miles, pass Chapman Campground, the location of a nature trail and reservoir. Continue on the paved Fryingpan Road until your odometer reads 32.3 miles. A sign for the Fryingpan Lakes is at right. Continue ahead as the road curves left and turns to gravel. A brown sign at right reads "Road #105, Sellar Meadow 2 miles, Hell Gate 6 miles, Hagerman Pass 10 miles." You are now on the Hagerman Pass Road, which makes a big loop east and north to broad Sellar Park. At 35.6 miles,

opposite the park, are signs for Diemer and Sellar Lakes. Far across the park is Mount Massive. The road next climbs above a valley, offering aerial peeks though the pines. At about 40 miles from Route 82, the nearby scene is dominated by rocks: boulders, rockfalls, stone cliffs—everywhere. The land falls away right of the road, offering huge vistas. At 42.0 miles look for beaver ponds below. At 43.0 miles, a sign points ahead for Ivanhoe Lake and left for Hagerman Pass. Take the left fork, drive a hundred feet and park at the Lyle Lake trailhead. A Forest Service register box and a map confirm your location.

Trail Route: Lyle Creek murmurs to the right of the path. The aspect is bright and open despite the many spruces and firs scattered about. Much of the summer this entire route is damp and flowery. Moisture-loving marsh marigolds and low willows tell the tale. Rounded granite shapes rest in the greenery, looking much like marbles forgotten by a playful giant. The creek splashes in mini-waterfalls as it meanders through this meadowy, subalpine terrain. Twice the trail crosses the water.

The route is clear as it heads northeast, first climbing a bit and then leveling out for more than a mile. As the trail bears north, or left, following the creek and valley, it mounts uphill more noticeably on its final approach to the broad bench holding Lyle Lake. A wooden sign stands at the near end of the water where a grassy expanse invites visitors to relax. Flower-lovers might look for gentian, fringed grass of parnasses and rosy paintbrush among the many blossoms here.

A trail circles the lake, inspiring exploration. The left shoreline may be 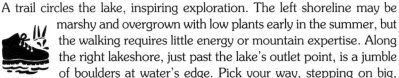 marshy and overgrown with low plants early in the summer, but the walking requires little energy or mountain expertise. Along the right lakeshore, just past the lake's outlet point, is a jumble of boulders at water's edge. Pick your way, stepping on big, stable stones. Five or six cairns serve as guides. A rocky promontory adorned with conifers makes a waterside picnic perch.

Hike Extension: For the adventurers in your party, Mormon Lake awaits, 1.75 miles away. The territory covered by this trail is remarkable for its beauty. And the large lake is a wilderness jewel. Less-traveled and less well-defined than the Lyle route, the Mormon trail covers varied, up-and-down terrain and treats hikers to visions of plunging valleys, countless ponds and towering sawtoothed peaks. Tiny pikas seem to be everywhere, crying "eehk" as you violate their space.

The dirt trail to Mormon is evident as it mounts a green slope directly across Lyle Lake. It begins at the end of the boulderfield on the lake's right side but can be approached from either direction. This initial uphill of 231 feet takes hikers to a splendid viewspot atop the peach-colored ridge surrounding Lyle. Mount Massive and its giant companions dominate the skyline behind you. Beyond here, it is downhill to Mormon.

The route travels beneath a west-facing mountainside. Walk this gentle path high above a verdant valley sprinkled with a multitude of ponds and cut by Cunningham Creek. Ahead, the pale, jagged mountains to the north separate these watery basins from basins cradling the Savage Lakes. Scout for cairns if the trail is faint, and scan ahead for its reappearance. Climb a little crest. After a small descent over stones, the route rounds a hillside and moves briefly into trees. Dampness from sidestreams encourages the flowering of chimingbells, red elephanthead and brookcress. An immense, sedimentary rock wall above the trail wears stripes of pink and gray.

Ramble through a flat meadow toward a desolate ridge. Exuberant plants may disguise the trail in early summer. Pass a little tarn at right. Then, as you edge a pond to your left, look for the sign announcing Mormon Lake ahead. While Lyle Lake's environs are lush and green, Mormon huddles below the meadow in a classic alpine bowl, embraced by stones. A long, gradual descent of about 100 feet carries you to this place of splendor and solitude. Mormon Creek flows northwest from its parent to merge with the

North Fork of the Fryingpan River. The lake is not stocked but contains naturally reproducing brook trout.

For another hike in the Fryingpan River Valley, see the description of the short Savages Lakes Trail in *The Aspen Dayhiker*.

Wilderness: Holy Cross   USGS map: Nast

Saint Benedict's Monastery

It is unexpected, this monastery in the mountains. But while its residents and its purpose seem eons removed from the contemporary Aspen scene, the monastery is perfectly fitted to its natural surroundings. For in the primordial wilderness of forest and tundra, one feels a pervasive quiet spirituality, a sense of underlying orderliness and rhythm, an absence of malice. So it is at Saint Benedict's.

In farming, too, there is a rhythm. And the fifteen Trappist monks working the land in the lovely Capitol Creek Valley incorporate this seasonal order into their lives of study, meditation and thrice-daily prayers. Established in the 1950s on the Staats and Hart ranches of old Snowmass, the monastery supports itself by raising hay and baking Snowmass Monastery Cookies, sold in local markets. The monks also offer their grounds, and their counseling skills if requested, to those in need of tranquility, solitude or contemplative days. A Retreat House will soon stand on a hillside above the monastery. Daily mass and prayers are open to the public.

The monks of Saint Benedict's belong to the venerable Cistercian Order established in 1098 by Saint Robert of Molesme. Their life style is based on the Rule of Saint Benedict, placing them in the Benedictine Family which reaches back to the sixth century.

Hardscrabble and
Williams Lakes Hike

GENERAL AREA:	Downvalley/Old Snowmass
TRAILHEAD:	25.6 miles from Mill & Main in Aspen
	22.3 miles from rodeo in Snowmass Village
HIKING DISTANCE:	1.0 mile round trip to Hardscrabble Lake
	4.0 miles round trip to Williams Lake
ELEVATION GAIN:	170 feet to Hardscrabble Lake
	855 feet to Williams Lake
LOW POINT:	9960 feet at trailhead
HIGH POINT:	10,815 feet at Williams Lake
HIGHLIGHTS:	Two lakes and a cascading stream
	Breathtaking scenery en route to trailhead
	Two hike extensions
FISHING:	Cutthroat trout in Hardscrabble Lake
	Brook trout in Williams Lake
NEARBY ATTRACTIONS:	Saint Benedict's Monastery
	Small town of Basalt on Fryingpan River

Comments: The stunning vista at the hike's start overlooks Capitol Creek Valley and Capitol Peak. The trail itself is woodsy and often buggy. Mosquito repellent is recommended. The lakes are favored by fishermen, but this is not a crowded place. The walk to Hardscrabble Lake is easy, and the climb to Williams Lake is especially beautiful as it parallels a cascading stream through cool, fragrant forest. Both lakes are sidetrips from the Hell Roaring Trail which ascends three miles to the ridge linking Mount Sopris and Capitol Peak. As both sidetrails are unmarked, be alert for the subtle landmarks described below.

The trip to Hardscrabble and Williams Lakes begins at the Capitol Lake parking area for those without a 4WD vehicle. Add 1.2 miles each way.

Aspen to Trailhead: Drive west from Aspen on Route 82, passing the Brush Creek Road turnoff for Snowmass Village. Continue 8.6 miles beyond this intersection to the sign for old Snowmass. Turn left from 82 at a gas station, drive 1.8 miles and bear right at the intersection of Snowmass Creek Road and Capitol Creek Road. Follow Capitol Creek Road past homes, llama ranches and a sign at left for Saint Benedict's Monastery. Head directly toward a rocky, snow-spotted expanse that stretches from Mount Sopris near Carbondale to Capitol Peak. The road deteriorates to dirt at 6.5 miles from Route 82. A mile beyond is a picturesque, tumbledown barn at right. About 9.0 miles from 82 the road becomes rough. This is about a mile short of the parking area for the Capitol Lake hike and 2.2 miles from the trailhead for Hardscrabble and Williams Lakes. Be cautious if your city car is new. An older vehicle or a truck will likely make it to the Capitol Lake trailhead. *Beyond that spot a nimble 4WD vehicle is needed.* Some of the road is steep and heavily rutted in the final 1.2 miles and 600 feet of elevation gain. A green metal gate and a grass-encircled pond mark the start of the trail.

Trail Route: A verdant, yawning valley, traversed by a twisting creek and beaver ponds, spreads below the cliff edge where the trail begins. Vast stands of pale aspen contrast with stately conifers attired in dark forest hues. Dominating everything is august Capitol Peak standing in the distance, its vertical ridges accentuated by snow. Mount Daly, to the left, shows an unfamiliar side to those who know its Snowmass Village face.

The wide earth and rock path is maroon-red and leads into a conifer forest, pleasantly aromatic but abuzz with biting insects in a wet summer. A wilderness sign stands just inside the woods. A ten-minute walk from the green gate brings you to the sidetrail to Hardscrabble Lake. Turn right at a large, reddish, lichen-covered rock embedded in the trail. Tall evergreens are to its right. There may or may not be a cairn atop the rock. The footpath dips and rises through spruces and firs and over roots before it drops to the small lake which reflects the green of its enclosing trees. The distance is very short. Mosses are everywhere in the woods, and grasses and white brookcress grow in the lake's shallows. Splashing trout interrupt the stillness. This intimate, pretty place is at an elevation of 10,130 feet.

Return to the main Hell Roaring Trail and hike for about one mile to the spur to Williams Lake. The route is a series of level areas alternating with uphills. Emerging from firs into aspens permits a lovely view into Capitol Creek valley below. Move again into firs as the trail rises and flattens out. The woods have a wonderful perfume and a carpet of needles. After this lengthy level section of trail, climb sharply up a knoll and pass through aspens in a bright spot. Many of the trees here are scarred by the gnawing of elk in winter. Descend into firs and look carefully to your right just as the path flattens at the bottom of the knoll. This is where you find the sidetrail to Williams Lake. It is not marked and is easy to miss.

The one-mile trail to the lake makes an initial steep drop from the Hell Roaring route and could be slippery if wet. As the path approaches a boggy, pond-filled area, marsh marigolds, globeflowers, chimingbells and brookcress make a flowery show. Cross a simple log and dirt footbridge over the bog. Snow may linger nearby in early summer. Another bridge, this one made of logs placed side to side, transports you across more water in this wet place. The water appears maroon from the red soil below. You may need to pick your footing carefully through this low area, making detours where necessary.

The trail starts gradually uphill and soon parallels a tumbling stream sparkling with white waterfalls. The stream has created the ponds below and makes a wonderful companion on the climb ahead. Occasional rocks along the trail grow mosses and flowers from small depressions. Organic matter created by lichens' interaction with rocks has generated tiny, unlikely garden plots. The trail steepens. Goatsbeard, a long, gray-green, hairlike moss, drapes from many conifers and dots the ground.

The cascading stream is exquisite in a big-snow year. There are numerous places to pause to enjoy its song and its fresh, cool beauty. Brookcress, common here, sprouts directly out of the water. The trail ascends and levels out several times as you walk under spruces and firs. Look for trees where porcupines have chewed off the outer bark to get to the tasty cambium layer underneath.

At the top of a rise you spy green Williams Lake, embraced by tall trees. Campsites are nearby, accessible from a path around the lake. The perimeter has many boulders and a few grassy openings rich with wildflowers. Above to the left is the

In the scenic **Snowmass and Capitol Creek Valleys** mineral exploration was not encouraging. More valuable than the limited ore was soil that supported basic crops such as potatoes, hay and small grains. Today the valleys' ranchers focus primarily on cattle and on modest herds of sheep, llamas and alpacas.

continuation of the Hell Roaring Trail, which overlooks this secluded spot from a red rocky outcropping visible from the lakeshore. Directly across the water is the high, undulating ridge reached by that trail. Elevation of the lake is 10,815 feet. Mosquitoes in a wet summer can be persistent, but insect repellent allows visitors to picnic, to fish or to explore. Picnickers are likely to be visited by bold gray jays, appropriately called "camp robbers," who aggressively seek handouts.

Hike Extension #1: Circle Williams Lake on a narrow footpath that edges the water, traveling in places over deadfall and rocks.

Hike Extension #2: If the weather is benign, those who wish to investigate this area further may return to the Hell Roaring Trail and hike uphill toward the rocky expanse joining Mount Sopris to Capitol Peak. The distance is about two miles. The steep route is atop a narrow ridge with many fine viewspots along the way. Upon reaching treelimit in a damp, level area, follow a red dirt path upward over tundra to a spacious pass with splendid views of little-traveled regions in the wilderness. Elevation here is 12,060 feet. See **The Aspen Dayhiker** for a detailed description of the Hell Roaring hike and the longer Capitol Lake hike.

Wilderness: Maroon Bells-Snowmass   USGS map: Capitol Peak

CRYSTAL RIVER

—+—‖◆‖—+—

Redstone
Avalanche Creek Hike
Rocky Mountain Mule Deer
Stinging Nettle
Crystal River, Beaver Lake & More

CRYSTAL RIVER REGION

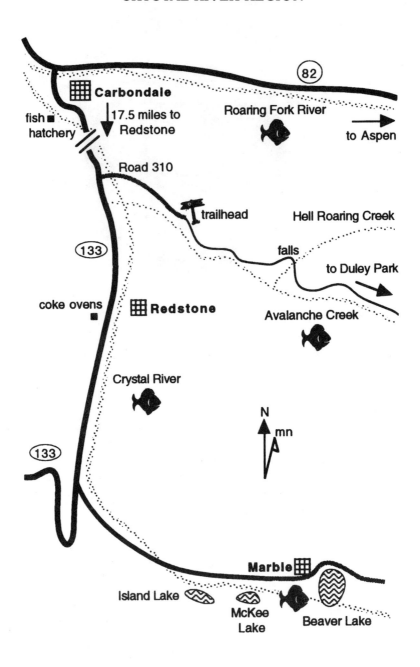

Redstone

J OHN CLEVELAND OSGOOD WAS AN UNUSUAL MINING MOGUL. PRAGMATIC, benevolent and cultured, he envisioned successful business linked to utopian ideas. Redstone was his invention and his experiment.

Founder of the Colorado Fuel & Iron Company, Osgood was among the ten richest Americans in the late 19th century. He purchased the coal claims in the Crystal River Valley in the 1880s and later determined to build a model community for the workers he would employ mining coal and converting it to coke for western smelting industries. Osgood hired a New York architect to help him design a tidy mountain village devoid of the haphazard ugliness typical of mining towns. The picturesque riverside site, overhung by flaming stone cliffs, sat a comfortable 12 miles from the grubby mining operations. A rail line carried men to work and coal to the coke ovens near town. By 1903 over 80 cottages lined Redstone's main street. Painted in pastel hues and equipped with the rare luxuries of running water and electricity, the small dwellings housed married employees.

Bachelors were comfortable in the Redstone Inn, a Tutor-style dormitory with 20 bedrooms, a barber shop, laundry, telephones, electric lights and reading rooms. Nearby were managers' homes and Osgood's own elegant 42-room mansion, an original creation of mixed ancestry known as Cleveholm Manor. Redstone had a hospital, school, modern bathhouse, company store, library and theatre. Osgood organized kindergartens and a variety of adult classes and clubs. This experiment in social progressivism was also intended to avoid labor troubles common to coal towns. Some miners did grumble about Osgood's strict rules of conduct, such as the requirement to bathe before appearing in public after working hours.

Redstone blossomed for a mere decade. The need for coke decreased as mining and smelting declined. Osgood, overextended financially, sought investment from eastern capitalists who took control of his enterprises. In 1909 the Coal Basin mines closed. Redstone was quiet, but Osgood maintained his beautiful home in its idyllic valley until he died in 1926. In modern times this sandstone "castle," with its splendid furnishings intact, has functioned as a bed and breakfast inn and a venue for weddings and special events. The Redstone Inn, enlarged from its dormitory days, welcomes guests today.

The deteriorating coke ovens, shaped vaguely like igloo row-houses, stand vacant and cold, but Redstone is quiet no more. Though its year-round residents may number a scant 100, Redstone is both a launch point for outdoor expeditions and a final destination for visitors. Working artists have supplanted miners in this tiny, one-street village on the Crystal River. Galleries and shops occupy some original cottages, and the Redstone Historic District is listed in the National Register of Historic Places.

Avalanche Creek Hike

GENERAL AREA:	Crystal River Valley
TRAILHEAD:	41.6 miles from Mill & Main in Aspen
	38.3 miles from rodeo in Snowmass Village
HIKING DISTANCE:	5.0 miles round trip to Hell Roaring Falls
ELEVATION GAIN:	850 feet
LOW POINT:	7310 feet at trailhead
HIGH POINT:	8160 feet at Hell Roaring Falls
HIGHLIGHTS:	Majestic Crystal River canyon
	Water everywhere
	Many wildflowers in airy woods
	Hike extension to Duley Park
FISHING:	Rainbow, cutthroat trout in Avalanche Creek
	Brook trout in Hell Roaring Creek
	Mountain whitefish in Crystal River
	Rainbow, brown, brook trout in Crystal River
NEARBY ATTRACTIONS:	Historic, charming village of Redstone
	Trout farm fishing in Crystal River
	Yule marble quarry and mill in Marble
	Rainbow trout in Marble's Beaver Lake

Comments: This is a lovely hike alongside water and over up-and-down terrain. The few steep sections are short, and the elevation gain is moderate. Hikers are almost everywhere serenaded by melodies from the creek, waterfalls and trickles. The trail is clear, making it difficult to get lost. The woods have a pleasant light, open quality; but on a cloudless day at this low elevation, the sun could feel hot. Many wildflowers adorn both woods and meadows. Travel with insect repellent and learn to recognize the stinging nettle plants alongside the path. Any comfortable athletic shoe is appropriate. Horses use this trail; move aside quietly if they approach.

Aspen to Trailhead: From Mill and Main in Aspen drive downvalley for 29.6 miles to the Route 133 intersection with Route 82 at Carbondale. Turn left onto 133 and proceed south into the Crystal River canyon, stunning with its flaming red walls. At 12.0 miles from 82, turn left onto Road 310. The gravel road crosses a bridge over the Crystal River. A sign reads "Narrow road. Not suitable for trailer traffic." At 1.7 miles a Forest Service sign points right for Avalanche Campground, one-half mile distant. Drive across shallow Bulldog Creek. At 2.5 miles from Route 133, park where a sign says "Wilderness Area Parking" at the end of the campground.

Trail Route: Enter the woods on a red dirt path where you immediately encounter a U.S. Forest Service sign and registry box. Walking is easy alongside magnificent Avalanche Creek, often gorged with sound and fury. Spruce trees, aspen daisies and bedstraw flourish here, as do early summer's fragrant roses. Bright openings near the water contribute to a cheerful atmosphere.

A wooden sign to the trail's right marks the Maroon Bells-Snowmass Wilderness boundary. The path climbs gradually, moving a little above the creek. Numerous sidestreams trickle across the path. In early July purple lupines are common among the serviceberries, junipers and oaks.

The trail narrows but is unmistakable. The forest is airy as you walk from conifers to aspens to conifers, treading on needles. Water music is still audible when you meander away from the creek to pass through a small meadow. Once back among the aspens, you meet a stream flowing down from the left. Scout for a narrow place to cross; this may involve a short detour in a year of heavy snowmelt. The trail continues to dip and rise and winds through a lush garden of ferns. Avalanche Creek continues to hurry by on the right. Just beyond the ferns is another little meadow. A sign on a tree near the water notes that this beautiful spot is an illegal campsite, closed for restoration.

Masses of cow parsnip bloom in the meadow. Flat white tops are everywhere. Just beyond, stinging nettles line both sides of the path. The trail climbs more steeply as you twist away from the creek; then it switchbacks quickly to parallel the water. The valley here is very narrow, and the creek has cut a deep gorge. As you ascend higher, the route again separates from the water in a quiet, mixed forest. Pass through an enormous ferny glade. A rock slide is on the right, and a sunset-colored rock face is above. Pikas skitter about, piping shrill warnings.

About 90 minutes to two hours into the hike is a post at left with a sign reading "Hell Roaring Trail No. 1960." This is the junction of Hell Roaring and Avalanche Creek trails, very near the place where Hell Roaring Creek plunges into Avalanche Creek. Drop steeply downhill. As creek sounds intensify, you see white, white water below. A layered red mountain peak topped by a fringe of conifers hovers above the deluge. Approach a bridge over the gorge carved by Hell Roaring Creek. The thunder of Hell Roaring Falls dominates this wonderful spot—an ideal place for a destination or a rest.

Hike Extension: To continue your hike to Duley Park, about three miles ahead, traverse the bridge and immediately ascend to a trail junction. The short uphill spur leads to a flat, aerial lookout above Avalanche Creek valley. This cliff edge is an inappropriate place for unrestrained children.

Return to the main trail and make a lengthy descent over rocks to the bank of Avalanche Creek. Many lovely picnic spots lie between here and Duley Park. The hike accompanies the creek upstream alongside rapids, whirlpools and pale blue-white frenzy. There is quiet drama as well: broad shallows, aquamarine pools, wildflower meadows, mossy glades, dulcet rivulets, overhanging crags, sawtoothed peaks, a snowy cirque. The undulating route abounds with uphills and downhills and concludes at 8450 feet of elevation.

In expansive Duley Park a few aspens bespeckle the meadow and denote its left boundary. Conifers skirt the right edge, and Avalanche Creek sparkles through the trees. A footpath twists through the park, moving toward faraway Avalanche Lake. Naked red ridges stand at left. Jagged mountains are poised in the distance, while on the right, horizontal bands of rocky cliffs alternate with bands of evergreens. Deer roam this peaceful field, and slender animal trails wind along the water.

For a more demanding hike in the Crystal River region, consult **The Aspen Dayhiker** for directions to Avalanche Pass.

Wilderness: Maroon Bells-Snowmass   USGS map: Redstone

Rocky Mountain Mule Deer
Everywhere and Nowhere

THEY DRINK FROM CHILL CREEKS AT DAWN, SHROUDED BY GHOSTLY FOG THAT billows over valley floors like a down comforter. They dissolve into woodlands at midday, as insubstantial as shadows. They materialize silently in meadows at dusk when the human eye begins to play tricks with reality. On wilderness trails the mule deer is everywhere and nowhere.

But many mountain visitors can expect to see these graceful animals. They are plentiful and sometimes bold enough to bound across manicured lawns or country roads. *Odocoileus hemionus hemionus*, the Rocky Mountain subspecies, is the largest mule deer in the West.

Mule deer are distinguished by and named for their sizable ears, five to six inches in length. These ears are mobile, moving independently and almost constantly. They express alarm when erect and forward, anger when flattened sideways, and fear when laid back against the neck.

A white rump and a narrow white tail tipped with black further differentiate the mule deer from other species. Also, a buck's antlers branch equally: Each separate beam forks into two tines, forming a distinctive Y-shape not characteristic of other deer. These antlers can spread to four feet in a mature male, are shed each winter and are used to joust with rivals during the autumn rut. Bucks commonly weigh 250 to 400 pounds while does are substantially smaller at 100 to 150 pounds.

To avoid heavy snow, mule deer migrate up and down mountainsides with the seasons. They travel alone or in small bands. Their coats change from yellow-brown or cinnamon in summer to gray-brown or sooty gray in winter. Fawns have their own camouflage: Their tan coats wear white spots to mimic the dappled light of the summer forest. Newborns have no scent, another natural protection.

Mule deer are browsers, found in open woods, along forest edges or in any brushy habitat. They prefer the twigs, buds and leaves of trees and shrubs but also graze on flowering plants, grasses and sedges. Acorns and apples may be eaten. Deer are ruminants, cud-chewers like cows.

Two-year-old does bear a single fawn, often followed by twins in successive pregnancies. The fawns, weighing about 10 pounds when born in early summer, are secreted for the first month and weaned in autumn. The cougar preys on mule deer; bobcats and coyotes take the weak, young or snowbound; automobiles extinguish other lives. Maximum life-span in the wild is 16 to 20 years.

> *"Animals are such*
> *agreeable friends;*
> *they ask no questions,*
> *they pass no criticisms."*
>
> —GEORGE ELIOT

Stinging Nettle
Bane or Bonanza?

BARE-LEGGED HIKERS, BEWARE. AMBUSH AWAITS YOU. ALONGSIDE DAMP trails, where the soil is rich and the vegetation is lush, flourishes an inconspicuous green plant with inconspicuous green flower clusters. Arched gracefully over the path from the weight of its foliage, the stinging nettle is perfectly poised to deliver its noxious prick to the unwary. Coarse hairs, actually tubes arising from a plant cell, break off when touched and, like hypodermic needles, pump formic acid into your skin. The burning chemical is the same used by biting ants. Relief can come from stroking smarting skin with the leaves of dock or mint, which often grow nearby. Even untreated, the sting will be gone within an hour or two, unless you have blithely marched, skin exposed, through a vast nettle encampment.

Attitudes have changed. Caesar's soldiers, shivering in the damp chill of conquered northern lands, planted the stinging nettle of their native Mediterranean. They rubbed their limbs with the weed to simulate a feeling of warmth. Medieval folks extracted the plant's juices to treat tuberculosis, brewed a tea of nettle leaves for toothaches and rheumatism, and used the seeds as a medicine for dysentery. Plant parts were once employed to make beer, to soothe burns and to cure nosebleeds.

Before the introduction of flax, nettle stem fibers were woven into cloth and twisted into twine. When Austria and Germany could not obtain cotton during World War I, nettles served as a substitute. And while these surreptitious stingers seem only an annoyance in today's world, they deserve some respect. Root extracts provide food coloring and a greenish yellow dye for wool. A natural pesticide is obtained from boiling the roots and leaves, and nettles in a compost pile can speed up decay.

Nettle sprouts, rendered harmless when cooked, are highly nutritious. And European physicians are experimenting with the nettle's value in treating prostate cancer and inflammations of the gall bladder.

Nettles flourish in spots along the Avalanche Creek Trail and the Ditch Trail to East Snowmass Creek. They are common along streams, irrigation ditches, roadsides and waste areas. Look for a green plant two to four feet tall with pairs of serrated, elongated leaves growing opposite on the main stem. Tiny, greenish flower clusters originate at the base of the leafstalks. *Urtica dioica* is entirely covered with brittle stinging hairs.

The Crystal River, Beaver Lake and More

WORD OF LEGENDARY FISHING ATTRACTS BOTH ARDENT VETERANS AND hopeful amateurs to the waters of the Crystal River Valley. While remote high-country streams and lakes summon adventurers, accessible Crystal River, Beaver Lake and Avalanche Creek make angling easy for fisherfolk with embryonic map and compass skills. And a foray into this place of fiery canyon walls and tumbled chunks of white marble can itself be satisfying.

While the Crystal River is without Gold Medal designation, it has bountiful devotees and an illustrious reputation. With native mountain whitefish and brown, brook and rainbow trout, there is much life beneath its hurried surface. The Crystal River Hatchery supplies Tasmanian and Belaire strains of rainbows, while the Rifle Falls Hatchery monitors browns, replenishing stock when needed. Over the summer months, 8700 twelve-inch rainbows are planted in the Crystal between the Roaring Fork and Redstone; 7500 more are added between Redstone and Marble; and another 3500 twelve-inchers are placed between Marble and Crystal City. Check with local outfitters about restrictions on catch. Approach the river in numerous spots from roadside parking on Route 133 or by foot trails.

Good family destinations lie south of Redstone. Between Route 133 and the village of Marble are two oversize ponds planted with rainbows. Known as Island Lake and McKee Lake, these two fishing holes are immediately right of the road. Island receives 800 twelve-inchers, and McKee receives 1000. On Marble's opposite boundary is large Beaver Lake. While 5200 twelve-inch rainbows are stocked here over the summer, extra fish are added in early spring and late fall. These are culled from hatchery brood stock and usually weigh two to six pounds. A visit to Marble could include a walk through the ruins of the old marble finishing mill in town or a drive or hike to the Yule Creek marble quarry, reopened in the 1990s.

North of Redstone is the tame Avalanche Creek Trail, which parallels a habitat for rainbow and cutthroat trout. Consult the hike description for the trailhead's location.

A commercial trout farm operates during summer months on the banks of the Crystal at Redstone. It supplies everything from gear to lessons to pan and trophy-size rainbows without imposing limits or requiring a license. This could be an introductory experience for children. A weekday visit to the Crystal River State Hatchery and Rearing Unit just south of Carbondale on Route 133 is yet another family excursion.

"It has always been my private conviction that any man who pits his intelligence against a fish and loses has it coming."

—JOHN STEINBECK

FISHING

The Aspen Fish Story
What's Under Water?
How Did They Get There?
What About a License?
Fishing Guide: Species by Location

"God never did make a
more calm, quiet, innocent
recreation than fishing.
It is a rest to the mind,
a cheerer of spirits,
a diverter of sadness,
a calmer of unquiet thoughts,
a moderator of passions...
and it begets habits of
peace and patience
in those who profess and
practice it."

—Sir Isaac Walton

The Aspen Fish Story

MARK TWAIN TRAVELED THE OLD WEST BY STAGECOACH, BUT HE NEVER packed into Aspen's mountains to dance a fishing line atop a whitewater stream. Had he ventured here, submitting himself to the intoxication of primal places, he might not have written, "There is no use in your walking five miles to fish when you can depend upon being just as unsuccessful near home."

The powerfully sensual beauty of Aspen's high country is reason enough to ply its waters. But more awaits the angler—especially the one intent on communing with cutthroat, brown, rainbow and brook trout. And here, fly fishing, not bait fishing, characterizes the sport. Local essays about its nuances are indistinguishable from poetry. Spirituality, obsession and ecstasy underlie the writers' words. And always, respect for the glistening quarry is palpable. Fly fishing hooks its practitioners.

Each region featured in this guide has numerous diversions for fishermen. With a few exceptions, the minihikes include water somewhere along the trail. Choose a region, collect your gear and explore.

In some locations, limits are imposed and catch-and-release policies apply. Consult with the area's many fishing outfitters for information, advice, supplies and licenses. Guides may be hired for both float and wade trips. Trout farms and private, stocked ponds charge a fee but do not require a fishing license. Go ahead. Get hooked.

What's Under Water?

Trout, that's what. Diminutive and burly. Naive and wary. Freckled and streaked in kaleidoscopic greens, browns, yellows and reds—the hues of mosses and verdigris, chestnuts and oatmeal, moonbeams and amber, apricots and blood. Trout, so artfully costumed by nature, suggest prisms, circus clowns and shell-studded sand.

Although they originated in the northeastern United States, **brook trout** are almost everywhere in Colorado's coldest waters. Stocked today less often than in the past, small brook trout cruise most chill creeks and some alpine lakes. Hardy, persistent and opportunistic, they are downright hard to discourage.

Native to California, showy **rainbow trout** are stocked heavily at present but are scheduled to be replaced in high alpine areas by the A+ strain of Colorado River cutthroat. The leaping rainbows flourish in temperatures more varied than those tolerated by other trout.

The **Colorado River cutthroat** is the only trout native to the Aspen area. The genetically pure, A+ strain is being planted in alpine wilderness waters locally and throughout northwestern Colorado. All other trout species occurring in this region were stocked here at one time. The Colorado River cutthroat is one of four subspecies of cutthroat original to this Rocky Mountain state. The yellowfin is extinct and the remainder are threatened: the greenback, the Colorado River and the Rio Grande. A red slash under the jaw characterizes all cutthroats.

Brown trout are not stocked within wilderness areas but are planted in the region's large rivers: the Roaring Fork, the Fryingpan and the Crystal. Browns were introduced to North America in 1883 and trace their roots back to Europe, north Africa and western Asia.

Lake trout, or Mackinaw trout, originated in the Great Lakes and require deep water and cool temperatures. They are not stocked locally today but are found in a few locations. The hybrid **splake**, a cross between lake trout and brook trout, is placed in Ruedi Reservoir but is not planted in other waters covered by this guide.

Ruedi also receives a generous annual allotment of **kokanee salmon**, a dwarf salmon of western lakes. This non-migratory variant of the Pacific sockeye matures to 10 to 16 inches and is known by additional names: little redfish, kickeninny and Kennerly's salmon.

A second Aspen native is the **mountain whitefish**. Never stocked, it reproduces well in both the Roaring Fork and Crystal rivers.

The native Greenback Cutthroat Trout has respect at last. Recently designated the **Colorado State Fish**, the greenback has supplanted that flashy California import, the rainbow. Found only east of Continental Divide, the greenback today is a "threatened" species, reclassified from its "endangered" status in 1993. This small, greenish-gold trout with black spots occupies only one-percent of its original habitat. Environmental factors, the stocking of competing fish and interbreeding have caused its precipitous decline, but serious recovery efforts are underway. They include establishing new wild populations from hatchery stocks.

How Did They Get There?

COLORADO WATERS HAVE BEEN STOCKED SINCE THE LATE 1800s, PROVIDING outdoorsmen and women with great sport. Of the 14 Division of Wildlife hatcheries in the state, only two are brood-stock hatcheries. One of these is in Glenwood Springs. Much time, expertise and money is invested in these special facilities. A major focus of the Glenwood State Hatchery and Rearing Unit is the restoration of the pure A+ strain of Colorado River cutthroat trout to its native habitat.

The Glenwood hatchery stocks a total of three to 3.5 million fish in northwestern Colorado's waters from late May until October. In July and August, 187 lakes in this same region receive 900,000 to one million trout. One-third of these are dropped 100 to 150 feet by airplane into remote alpine lakes—lakes often encircled by a jumble of ragged peaks. This tricky aerial stocking practice is employed in alternate years in most locations and deposits small trout, one to four inches long. Large trout, those 10 inches or more in length, are planted by truck in more accessible locations over a period of three to four months.

The rivers in this guide are partially stocked by the Crystal River and Rifle Falls hatcheries which, like Glenwood, are managed by the Colorado Division of Wildlife.

What About a License?

COLORADO DESIGNATES NO "SEASON" FOR FISHING. A LICENSE IS REQUIRED all year for anyone age 15 and over. However, the first weekend in June is set aside for free fishing for two days. No license is needed. Fees in 1995 were set at $20.25 per year for an adult resident, $40.25 per year for a nonresident, and $5.25 for a one-day license for anyone. While no fee is charged to fishermen under age 15, bag limits are halved.

Licenses may be purchased at all City Markets and at the many fishing outfitters in the Roaring Fork Valley, including Taylor Creek in Basalt and both upvalley Oxbow Outfitting companies. Licenses are also available in Snowmass Village at Gene Taylor Sports and in Aspen at the Miners Building, Carl's Pharmacy, Aspen Sports and Pomeroy Sports.

Fishing Guide: Species by Location

	Region	Page	Rainbow	Brook	Cutthroat	Brown	Lake	Whitefish	Salmon	Splake
Lakes										
Anderson	LC	139	x							
Beaver	CR	178	x							
Crater	MB	62			x					
Hardscrabble	D	163			x					
Independence	IP	130		x						
Island	CR	178	x							
Linkins	IP	127	x							
Lost Man	IP	130		x	x					
Lyle	D	159		x			x			
Maroon	MB	62	x							
McKee	CR	178	x							
Mormon	D	159		x						
Petroleum	LC	139	x							
Weller	M	110	x							
Williams	D	163		x						

Key to Regions: A = Aspen; CC, Castle Creek; CR, Crystal River; D, Downvalley; IP, Independence Pass; LC, Lincoln Creek; M, Midway; MB, Maroon Bells; SV, Snowmass Village.

Fishing Guide: Species by Location (continued)

	Region	Page	Rainbow	Brook	Cutthroat	Brown	Lake	Whitefish	Salmon	Splake
Reservoirs										
Chapman	D	157	x							
Grizzly	LC	146	x							
Lost Man	M	120	x							
Ruedi	D	155	x				x		x	x
Rivers										
Crystal	CR	178	x	x		x		x		
Fryingpan	D	155	x	x		x				
Roaring Fork	A	56	x	x		x		x		
Creeks										
Avalanche	CR	171	x		x					
Brush	SV	93	x	x						
Castle	CC	77	x							
Hell Roaring	CR	171		x						
Hunter	A	42			x					
Lincoln	LC	146	x							
W. Maroon	MB	62		x						
E. Snowmass	SV	89	x							

Key to Regions: A = Aspen; CC, Castle Creek; CR, Crystal River; D, Downvalley; IP, Independence Pass; LC, Lincoln Creek; M, Midway; MB, Maroon Bells; SV, Snowmass Village.

Bibliography

Armstrong, David M. *Rocky Mountain Mammals*. Boulder: Colorado Associated University Press, 1987.

Auger, Raymond N., and Pamela Hepburn. *Aspen Trail Guide*. Aspen: [n.p.] 1971.

Bright, William. *Colorado Place Names*. Boulder: Johnson Books, 1993.

Brown, Robert L. *Ghost Towns of the Colorado Rockies*. Caldwell: The Caxton Printers, Ltd., 1968.

Burt, William H., and Richard P. Grossenheider. *A Field Guide to the Mammals*, 3rd ed. New York: Houghton Mifflin Company, 1980.

Carter, Jack L. *Trees and Shrubs of Colorado*. Boulder: Johnson Books, 1988.

Craighead, John J., Frank C. Craighead, Jr., and Ray J. Davis. *Rocky Mountain Wildflowers*. Boston: Houghton Mifflin Company, 1963.

Danielson, Clarence L., and Ralph W. Danielson. *Basalt: Colorado Midland Town*. Boulder: Pruett Press Inc., 1965.

dePaola, Tomie. *The Legend of the Indian Paintbrush*. New York: G.P. Putnam's Sons, 1988.

Duft, Joseph F., and Robert K. Moseley. *Alpine Wildflowers of the Rocky Mountains*. Missoula: Mountain Press Publishing Company, 1989.

Filisky, Michael. *Peterson First Guides to Fishes*. Boston: Houghton Mifflin Company, 1989.

Frey, Ruth, and Peter Frey. *The Aspen Dayhiker*. Evanston: Brush Creek Books, 1993.

Hall, Alan. *The Wild Food Trail Guide*. New York: Henry Holt and Company, 1976.

Hubbard, Fran. *Animal Friends of the Rockies*. Fredericksburg: Awani Press, 1970.

Keilty, Maureen. *Best Hikes With Children in Colorado*. Seattle: The Mountaineers, 1991.

Lehner, Ernst, and Johanna Lehner. *Folklore and Odesseys of Food and Medicinal Plants*. New York: Tudor Publishing Company, 1962.

Little, Elbert L. *The Audubon Society Field Guide to North American Trees - Western Region*. New York: Alfred A. Knopf, 1990.

Living Art Company. *Aspen: The 100 Year High.* New York: Books in Focus, Inc., 1980.

Loewer, Peter. *The Wild Gardener.* Harrisburg: Stackpole Books, 1991.

Marsh, Charles S. *People of the Shining Mountains.* Boulder: Pruett Publishing Company, 1982.

Martin, Laura C. *Wildflower Folklore.* Old Saybrook: The Globe Pequot Press, 1984.

Nelson, Ruth Ashton. Revised by Roger L. Williams. *The Handbook of Rocky Mountain Plants.* Niwot: Roberts Rinehart Publishers, 1992.

Nevin, David. *The Old West: The Expressmen.* Ed. George Constable. New York: Time-Life Books, 1974.

Ono, R. Dana, James D. Williams, and Anne Wagner. *Vanishing Fishes of North America.* Washington: Stone Wall Press, Inc., 1983.

O'Rear, John, and Frankie O'Rear. *The Aspen Story.* New York: A.S. Barnes and Company, Inc., 1966.

O'Shea, Michael. *The New Aspen Area Trail Guide.* Aspen: [n.p.] 1975.

Pearce, Sarah J., and Roxanne Elfin. *Guide to Historic Aspen and the Roaring Fork Valley.* Evergreen: Cordillera Press, Inc., 1990.

Pettit, Jan. *Utes: The Mountain People.* Colorado Springs: Century One Press, 1982.

Rohrbough, Malcolm J. *Aspen: The History of a Silver Mining Town 1879-1893.* New York: Oxford University Press, 1986.

Russo, Ron. *Mountain State Mammals.* Berkeley: Nature Study Guild, 1991.

Shikes, Robert. Vice-Chairman of Pathology, University of Colorado School of Medicine. Lecture "Mining Camp Medicine." Given Biomedical Institute, Aspen, Colorado, September 4, 1994.

Shoemaker, Leonard C. *Place Names In — Roaring Fork Valley.* Glenwood Springs: [n.p.] 1970.

Strickler, Dee. *Alpine Wildflowers.* Columbia Falls: The Flower Press, 1990.

Walden, Howard T. *Familiar Freshwater Fishes of America.* New York: Harper & Row, 1964.

Whitaker, John O., Jr. *The Audubon Society Field Guide to North American Mammals.* New York: Alfred A. Knopf, 1980.

Wyrick, Ken, and J.B. Ware. *Hiking Guide to Aspen.* Aspen: Aspen Editors, Inc., 1978.

Young, Robert G., and Joann W. Young. *Colorado West: Land of Geology and Wildflowers.* Grand Junction: [n.p.] 1984.

The Author

RUTH FREDERICKS FREY acquired her fondness for Rocky Mountain trails in the mid-1970s and now makes her summer home in the Aspen area. With her husband Peter, she wrote *The Aspen Dayhiker*, introduced by Brush Creek Books in 1993. An amateur naturalist and a quilter, Ruth is a new convert to snowshoeing, thereby extending the hiking season. Writing represents a second career, succeeding responsibilities as a mother, teacher and college administrator.

The Artist

DONNA CURRIER is a free-lance illustrator who began her professional career in Denver where she designed advertisements, worked as a courtroom artist and created graphics for television. Now in the Midwest, she applies her skills to a wide range of projects from wall murals to books, including *The Aspen Dayhiker*. Donna volunteers her talents and extra hours to numerous youth organizations and retreats with her family to a Wisconsin lakeside cottage each summer.

BRUSH CREEK BOOKS
1317 Livingston Street • Evanston, IL 60201 • (708) 328-2844

Please mail ASPEN ON FOOT to the address below:

Name _____

Address _____

City/State/Zip _____

Telephone _____

I wish to order _____ copies of ASPEN ON FOOT

I enclose $14.95 per book   total $_____

I enclose $2.50 per book for postage & packaging   total $_____

TOTAL ENCLOSED $_____

- -

BRUSH CREEK BOOKS
1317 Livingston Street • Evanston, IL 60201 • (708) 328-2844

Please mail ASPEN ON FOOT to the address below:

Name _____

Address _____

City/State/Zip _____

Telephone _____

I wish to order _____ copies of ASPEN ON FOOT

I enclose $14.95 per book   total $_____

I enclose $2.50 per book for postage & packaging   total $_____

TOTAL ENCLOSED $_____